HEALING EVE

An Inner Healing Programme for Daughters in Christ

Dee Edwards-Julien

Grosvenor House
Publishing Limited

The right of Dee Edwards-Julien to be identified as the author of this
work has been asserted in accordance with Section 78
of the Copyright, Designs and Patents Act 1988

The book cover is copyright to Dee Edwards-Julien

This book is published by
Grosvenor House Publishing Ltd
Link House
140 The Broadway, Tolworth, Surrey, KT6 7HT.
www.grosvenorhousepublishing.co.uk

A CIP record for this book
is available from the British Library

ISBN 978-1-83615-076-3
eBook ISBN 978-1-83615-077-0

This book is not intended as a substitute for
medical advice or treatment. Any person with
a condition requiring medical attention should consult
a qualified medical practitioner, pastor or suitable therapist.

Acknowledgements

The author gives all praise to Christ the King, our intercessor, who in a vision revealed to me how He knelt before Abba Father to plead for my life to be spared. I am no longer dead, but I am alive in Christ.

I am in awe of the Holy Spirit, my teacher (always on standby) to lead me in all truth. Thank you.

I thank Elohim for blessing me with my two beautiful children, Melissa and Tyrone, who are both a source of inspiration and support every day. I give thanks for you both every day!

For my parents, Tony Julien and Geraldine Edwards for teaching me resilience, tenacity, and to never give up (unless Christ tells me otherwise)!

I pray that my children, Tyrone and Melissa, along with my brother, sisters, nieces, nephews, come to know the love of Christ for themselves and experience the saving grace of Christ Yeshua.

For the wonderful ladies who volunteered themselves for my 'Healing Eve' online pilot course workshop 2021/22. Your feedback and encouragement have been a blessing to me and spurred me on to write the course in book form. You are all amazing women of God.

For my church families: Lordship Lane Baptist Church (Dulwich), where I gave my life to Christ and where 'Healing Eve' was birthed with the support of the members.
Rye Lane Baptist Church: your ministry has played a significant part in my healing. Thank you.

For Naomi Sinani who has blessed me with her time and her 'eagle eye' for proofreading and administration. You are an extremely talented woman. It's time you believed it! May the Lord bless you abundantly and give you the desires of your heart.

Thank you to Jacqueline Reid and Pastor Thomas Joseph for your support, prayer and wise counsel.

For Tia Wedderburn, who did such a wonderful job designing the book cover. You are extremely talented.

Finally, I would like to thank Spring Harvest 2024 for blessing me with the funding that has enabled me to publish *Healing Eve*. Spring Harvest 2024 was life-changing!

Finally, to all the women and girls all over the world who will read and complete this workbook. I pray that you will allow the love of Christ to heal and transform you so that you may fulfil the destiny Christ has for you. Amen.

Dedication

I dedicate this book to Melissa and Tyrone, my two children, who are my source of joy, laughter, and determination. The Lord allowed me to draw a line in sand and raise you both in love and gratitude. When I feel downtrodden, the Lord uses you both to make me smile and spur me on. Melissa, thank you for your loving encouragement and the many belly-laughs you give me. You are both my bundles of love.

Forward

In 2011, I gave my life to Christ and began the fantastic journey of answering Christ's call. I was born and raised in London by parents of St. Lucian descent. They had journeyed to London to support rebuilding the 'motherland'. The 70's were tough for us. I witnessed first-hand the struggle my parents had with their mental health and well-being due to being mistreated by white citizens. Their pain and disappointment manifested as weekly domestic violence incidents, alcoholism, and a household that was always on 'high alert'. Such an environment opened the door to a 'spirit of rejection' because of the colour of our skin. White people punished us for being different. A heightened sense of rejection, loss, and discrimination very much plagued my life. Others like me, just didn't fit in.

As a child, I just wanted to be accepted. The spirit of rejection was evident in my life, and I coped by wearing a mask. My mask was laughing and joking, enabling me to make friends easily.

Whilst I attended church every Sunday, it was a ceremonial activity that took place on a Sunday and an opportunity to wear nice clothes.

Fast forward 40 years, I now realise what it truly means to have a relationship with and in Christ. In relationship with Christ, I have learned that you are in the world but not of it (John 15:19-20). Yahweh uses me to share his Son in a particular way with his broken daughters, (Ephesians 1:11-23). Yahweh prepared me to be a daughter, mother, aunt, friend, therapist, teacher, and supervisor. He uses me to help women and young girls to understand their calling in Christ. This workbook will deepen your relationship with the Father, Son, and Holy Spirit (if you desire it).

Inspired by the Holy Spirit to write this workbook in 2021, I was also instructed to complete the programme myself. As I delved deeper into the programme, I found myself in tears, overwhelmed by the emotional journey it took me on. The Holy Spirit reminded me that I could not authentically write this book unless I, too, continued in my healing and deliverance with Christ. There were still areas of my life closed off to Christ. So, my prayer for you is that you will allow Christ to do the work that He had begun in you since the foundations of this world, so that you may be wholly blameless before Him when you see Him face-to-face. Amen.

For more information on my 'Healing Eve' events and programmes, please visit www.deeedwardsjulien.co.uk.

vi

CONTENTS

Introduction:

How to Use this Workbook

This is an inner healing programme for daughters in Christ who desire to address their own issues of low self-esteem and self-worth. It has three aims:

- To help you better understand personal issues from a Christ-centred perspective.
- To teach you the practical skills (underpinned by scripture) that will lead to your transformation.
- To realise your calling and walk in the plan Yahweh has for you.

How is the workbook structured?

The 'Healing Eve – An Inner Healing Programme for Daughters in Christ', will help you understand how low self-esteem and self-worth originated at the fall, and how Satan and his army seek to:

- **Keep you away from your heavenly Father.**
- **Prevent you from experiencing Abba Father's love and blessing.**
- **Prevent you from experiencing the true love of Christ.**
- **Keep you from your healing (spirit, mind, and body) and**
- **Keep from your calling and the wondrous plan Yahweh has for you.**

Our heavenly Father wants you to make the changes in your life so that you begin to feel more confident, kind, and accepting towards yourself and others. He wants to pour into you so your overflow can assist others and bring people to Christ.

These programmes are designed to help you work through these topics yourself, or with a small group of mature or younger women in your local church. I would strongly suggest that you have at least eight to 12 participants in any group. Larger groups can negatively affect the intimacy and safety between group members.

Worksheets & Templates

With plenty of questionnaires, worksheets, and practical exercises, the eight modules together make up a structured course.

HOW TO COMPLETE THIS COURSE

Who is the programme for?

This programme is specifically aimed at Christian women seeking a deeper and more intimate relationship with Abba Father through Christ Yeshua and the power of the Holy Spirit. However, you may wish to invite friends, family, or non-believers to work through the programme together.

How to study this programme

I strongly recommend that you dedicate a minimum of a week to each module. You can take a day out for your intimate time with Christ or set aside an hour a day. Remember, you will reap what you sow (Galatians 6:7). If you put in minimal commitment, you will reap little benefit.

How long will the programme take?

Healing Eve is designed as a weekly programme lasting approximately eight weeks, with each unit requiring approximately two to three hours to complete (if completed alone). The course can take up to 16 weeks or more if completed as a group.

Would you recommend completing the programme alone or within a women's group?

Completing this programme needs to be entirely led by Christ. Please listen to His voice if He requires you to complete it alone. On page xi, I give very clear guidelines for completing this as a group. You can also visit my website if your church group wishes to book a facilitator to deliver your programme or to train a group leader to become a qualified facilitator. For more information, visit: www.deeedwardsjulien.co.uk

What topics will the programme cover?

Throughout these eight weeks, this programme will explore eight topics that affect the lives of Christian women. More can be found on the next few pages.

What materials will I need?

Access to a Bible while completing this programme is compulsory. I recommend either the King James version and/or a study Bible. A good-sized journal to take notes and complete your homework tasks would also be helpful.

Modules

Module One explores:

- Foundations of intimacy with Christ
- Blocks to intimacy with Christ
- Exploring significant relationships
- Blocks to intimacy with others

Module Two explores:

- The biblical definition of low self-esteem and self-worth
- The generational curse of low self-worth and self-esteem originating at the fall, and how it has directly affected women
- How low self-esteem and low self-worth affect daughters in Christ today
- What keeps low self-esteem going?
- Our identity in Christ

Module Three explores:

- What is rejection?
- Understanding the roots of rejection
- The impact of rejection at the fall, and how it impacted women
- The generational curse of rejection and its outworking in your life

Module Four explores:

- What is a 'spirit of fear'?
- How fear affects our lives
- The generational curse of fear and its outworking in your life

Part Five explores:

- What is a personality mask?
- Why do you wear a mask?
- The impact of wearing a mask with Christ
- The impact of wearing masks in relationships
- Allowing Christ to remove our mask

Part Six explores:

- What is anger?
- The root(s) of anger
- Righteous and unrighteous anger
- How anger has affected your life
- How to safely express your anger to others

Part Seven explores:

- What is true repentance?
- What is true forgiveness?
- The spiritual, mental, and physical cost of unforgiveness
- Who I need to forgive?

Part Eight explores:

- The origins of gifts and talents
- Barriers to walking in your calling
- How to walk in your calling
- Sharing your healing testimony

Want to work with a group?

It is important to note that when facilitating a 'Healing Eve' group, you must have a strong foundation in Christ. It is extremely beneficial if you are a qualified counsellor and group facilitator. These complementary qualifications are extremely important to maintain the safety and confidentiality of the group.

This programme encourages sharing intimate things about yourself, listening without judgement, and confessing sinful behaviours. If you feel unable to trust other programme participants, I recommend you complete this programme alone. During the year, 'Healing Eve' will hold open courses, and if you wish to work with other sisters in Christ that you have no previous connection with, please visit our website for up-and-coming events at www.deeedwardsjulien.co.uk

Need extra support?

You may find that in completing this course, you need additional emotional support. I would encourage you to seek out the support of a qualified Christian counsellor or speak to a trusted brother or sister in Christ.

Group Contract

When completing this programme as a group, it is essential that a group contract is drawn up and that all participants agree with its contents. There should be no voting to agree on issues; there should be a unanimous consensus about maintaining confidentiality, boundaries, and the group's safety throughout the programme.

If you choose to share something personal, it is important that you are comfortable with disclosing this information. The facilitator will not force you to share anything you are uncomfortable with. Areas for negotiation in your group contract can be as follows: confidentiality, timekeeping, mobile phone, recording sessions, speaking time, feedback, etc.

Please note: the only time when a group participant is permitted to break confidentiality is when a course participant has disclosed:

- Harm to self and others.
- Knowledge and/or participation in acts of terrorism.
- Knowledge and/or participation in drug trafficking.

Getting the most from the course

These modules are practical tools. So, write in the spaces in your workbook, underline, highlight things, write comments and respond to questions in the margins. When you finish with a workbook, it should be full of notes to look back on.

Here are some tips to help you get the most from each unit.

- Take your time and go at your own pace. This workbook will sometimes ask you to reflect on painful issues around your past and current experiences. However, if some of these painful issues are distressing you, I would strongly encourage you to work these through with Christ Yeshua and the support of a Christian counsellor. The rewards will be life changing.

- Please be prepared to invest time in doing the practical exercises – you can just set aside one hour each day if you can. You can divide this into 30-minute chunks, with 30 minutes of reflective study in the day and evening. Please prayer before your sit down to study.

- Use the 'Thoughts and Reflections' section at the back of the workbook to write down anything you feel the Lord is speaking to you about. It is important to listen to the Holy Spirit.

- Please do your best to answer all the questions and do the exercises, even if you need to return to them later. We can get stuck when we are exploring painful issues. If this happens, pray and ask the Holy Spirit for guidance and revelation. Put the workbook aside, pray, worship, and return to it when you feel more settled.

- You can work through this workbook alone, but you may find it helpful if you work through the modules with a Christian women's group. The support of a professionally facilitated group helps to encourage members to persevere, to feel supported and held when a group member is finding it difficult to engage.

- You can re-read the workbook or revisit exercises (in fact, I encourage it). The Holy Spirit will direct you to areas in the workbook that may have been missed or overlooked. You may get more out of it once you have prayerfully had a chance to reflect.

- Each unit builds on what has already been covered. So, what you learn in one unit will help you when you come to the next. I strongly encourage you to follow each unit systematically, step by step, rather than dipping in and out.

I pray this programme will transform you and your life more than you can imagine. Remember, Christ wants to heal your broken heart and set you free.

MODULE 1
INTIMACY WITH CHRIST

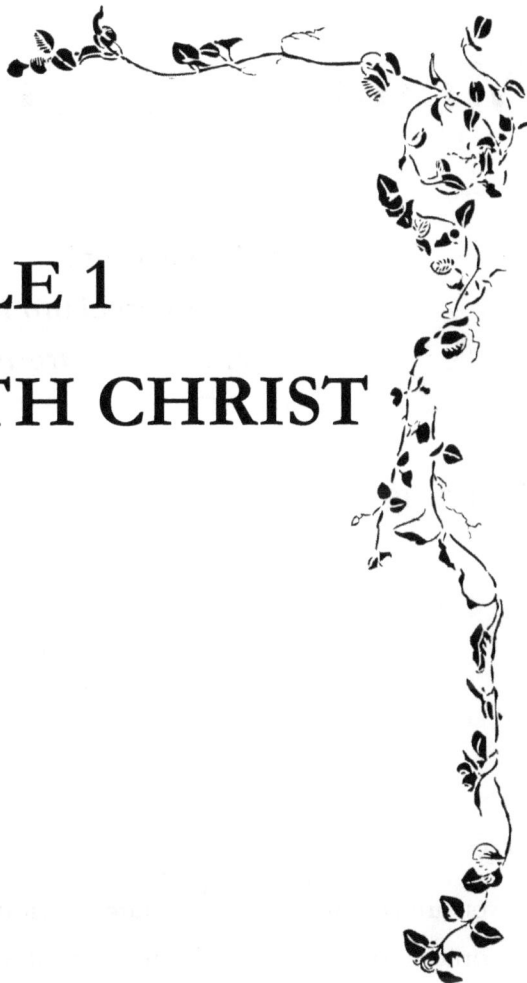

Module 1: Intimacy with Christ

"He has sent me to bind up the brokenhearted,
to proclaim freedom for the captives
and release from darkness for the prisoners"
Isaiah 61:1 (KJV)

Opening Prayer:

Group Contract:

If you are completing this programme within a group, I suggest that you remind participants of the importance of remaining committed to the group contract. Revisit the contract at the start of each session to ensure the group's safety. The group must adhere to it!

Module 1 Reflection

If working as a group, set aside 15-30 minutes every time you meet to share your reflections after each session. Please keep to time boundaries.

Module Aims:

In this module, you will be exploring 'Intimacy with Christ'.

Module Outcomes:

By the end of Workbook 1, you will be able to:
- Explore what it means to be in an intimate relationship with Christ Yeshua.
- Define your personal experience of intimacy with Christ.
- Define your personal experience of your relationship with Christ.
- Identify three or more of your blocks to intimacy with Christ.
- Reflect on your learning in your journal.

Session 1: This week we will be exploring 'Intimacy with Christ'.

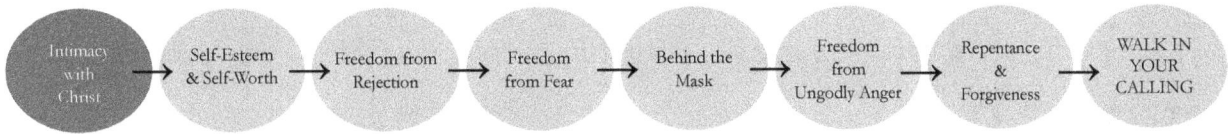

Module 1: What I hope to gain from completing this programme.

Before we get started...

Alone or in pairs, write down the answers to the following questions:

1. What do I hope to gain from the *'Healing Eve'* programme?

_____

_____

_____

_____

_____

2. What do I hope to learn about my relationship with Christ Yeshua?

_____

_____

_____

_____

_____

3. What support might I need from others or the group?

_____

_____

_____

_____

_____

Intimacy with Jesus

John 15:1-11 King James Version (KJV)

"I am the true vine, and my Father is the husbandman.

2 Every branch in me that beareth not fruit he taketh away: and every branch that beareth fruit, he purgeth it, that it may bring forth more fruit.

3 Now ye are clean through the word which I have spoken unto you.

4 Abide in me, and I in you. As the branch cannot bear fruit of itself, except it abide in the vine; no more can ye, except ye abide in me.

5 I am the vine, ye are the branches: He that abideth in me, and I in him, the same bringeth forth much fruit: for without me ye can do nothing.

6 If a man abide not in me, he is cast forth as a branch, and is withered; and men gather them, and cast them into the fire, and they are burned.

7 If ye abide in me, and my words abide in you, ye shall ask what ye will, and it shall be done unto you.

8 Herein is my Father glorified, that ye bear much fruit; so shall ye be my disciples.

9 As the Father hath loved me, so have I loved you: continue ye in my love.

10 If ye keep my commandments, ye shall abide in my love; even as I have kept my Father's commandments, and abide in his love.

11 These things have I spoken unto you, that my joy might remain in you, and that your joy might be full."

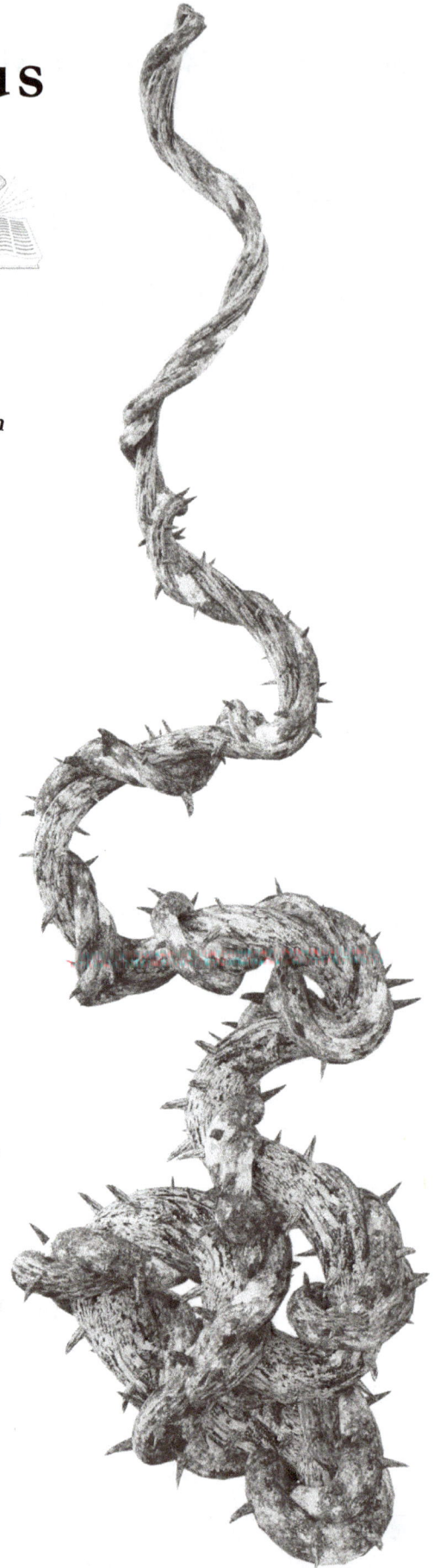

Personal Reflection Point:

Exercise 1

A. How does this piece of scripture speak to you?

_____

_____

_____

_____

_____

_____

_____

B. What does this piece of scripture demonstrate to you about the relationship between Abba Father, Christ Yeshua, and you?

_____

_____

_____

_____

_____

_____

_____

Intimacy Lost...

The Bible depicts the failure of a grape crop as evidence of God's judgment on his people (Isaiah 18:5).

John 15:1-11 gives insight to the level of intimacy the vinedresser (Yahweh) has with us through His son, Christ Yeshua; we abide in Christ and Christ abides in us. Our Father in Heaven wants to enjoy the fruits of his labour (us), so he tends to his grapes (us) to prune us and make His crop fruitful.

A gardener must tend their plants regularly to yield a harvest. The gardener must know what is yielding a crop and what isn't. The gardener has an intimate relationship with their crops; how else will they know how to care for them? This is the intimacy that Elohim wants with His offspring.

Where there is no intimacy with Christ, the result is frustration and a struggle with sin. During this separation, Abba Father cannot enjoy the fruit (us) He has tended to. With no intimacy with our Father in heaven, our fate (like sinful Israel) is a life of poverty, futility, frustration, and death (Deuteronomy 28:39). In Habakkuk 1:13, we are told that Yahweh cannot abide sin. The Bible says we will labour in vain (Psalm 127:1), whilst the righteous life produces abundant harvest and celebration with our Lord and King. For the vinedresser to care for us, tend to us, prune us, water us, speak over us, bless us, chastise us (I could on), we must be willing to abide in His vine. That vine is Christ Yeshua. Furthermore the Apostle Paul reminds believers in Romans 4:7 that Christ covers our sins if we abide in Him and follow His commandments.

Remember that intimacy was lost when Adam and Eve sinned against Yahweh. Adam and Eve knew they had sinned against the Lord and had eaten of the fruit that the Lord had forbidden them to eat (Genesis 3). A demonstration of this intimacy can be found in Genesis 3:8 (KJV) 'And they heard the voice of the Lord God walking in the garden in the cool of the day: and Adam and his wife hid themselves from the presence of the Lord God amongst the trees of the garden.'

This verse highlights the fellowship and intimacy our Lord has with His creation. Before Adam and Eve sinned, they were an intimate part of the vine. They met with the Lord in the Garden of Eden. Through their disobedience, the closeness of the relationship had gone. Yahweh instructed Adam and Eve to leave the home He had created for them. They were never allowed to return to their abundant home. Yahweh served them with an eviction notice.

Although the Lord made provisions for them outside of the garden, the relationship between Yahweh and man appeared distant. After 'the fall', we observe that Adam and Eve have no face-to-face relationship with the Lord (Genesis 3:8). We do not see another mention of Yahweh walking amongst Adam and Eve. We are informed in John 1:18 that "No 'man' has seen the Father except for His only begotten Son, which is in the bosom of the Father." So why was this different in the Garden of Eden?

Following the 'fall' of Adam and Eve, the intimacy was lost when they sinned against Yahweh. In turn, all power and rulership over the earth given to Adam and Eve was transferred to Satan.

Their 'fall' allowed every manner of unclean spirits to enter and influence and shape the world we live in today. These unclean spirits have a mandate to '...kill, steal and destroy' Yahweh's creation (John 10:10). It will be some 3000-plus years for humanity to be redeemed, through the birth, death and resurrection of Christ Yeshua. From this point, we were invited to restore our relationship with Yahweh through Christ Yeshua, as our sins were finally atoned for.

In our next exercise, we will explore what 'relationship' personally means to us, whether spiritual, physical, or mental. We will explore both the world view and the heavenly view of relationships and how we live our lives in relation to these opposing views.

Exercise 2

Relationships

Jot down all the words associated with the word 'relationship'.

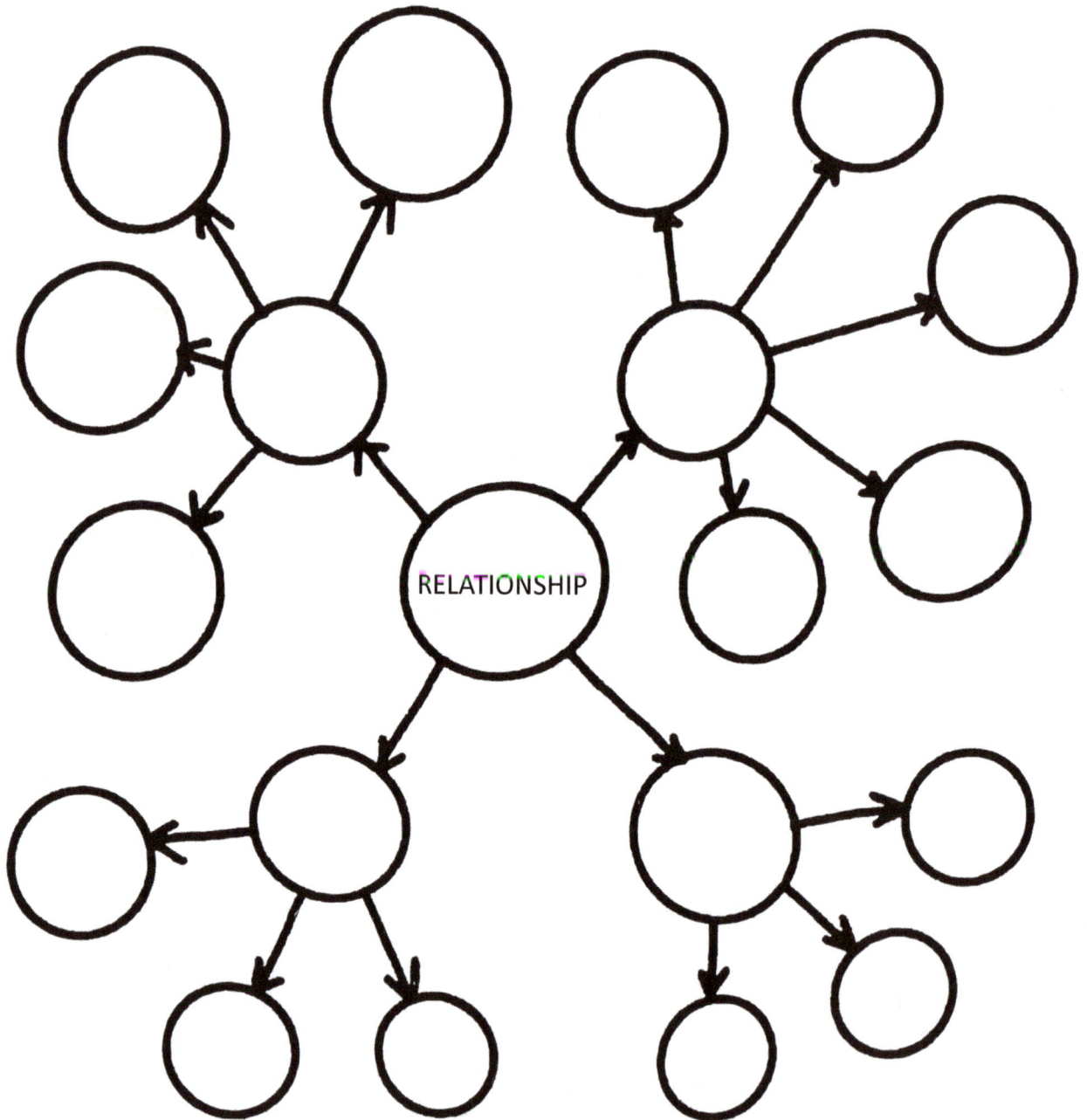

RELATIONSHIP

Personal Reflection Point

Where is my relationship with Christ Yeshua?

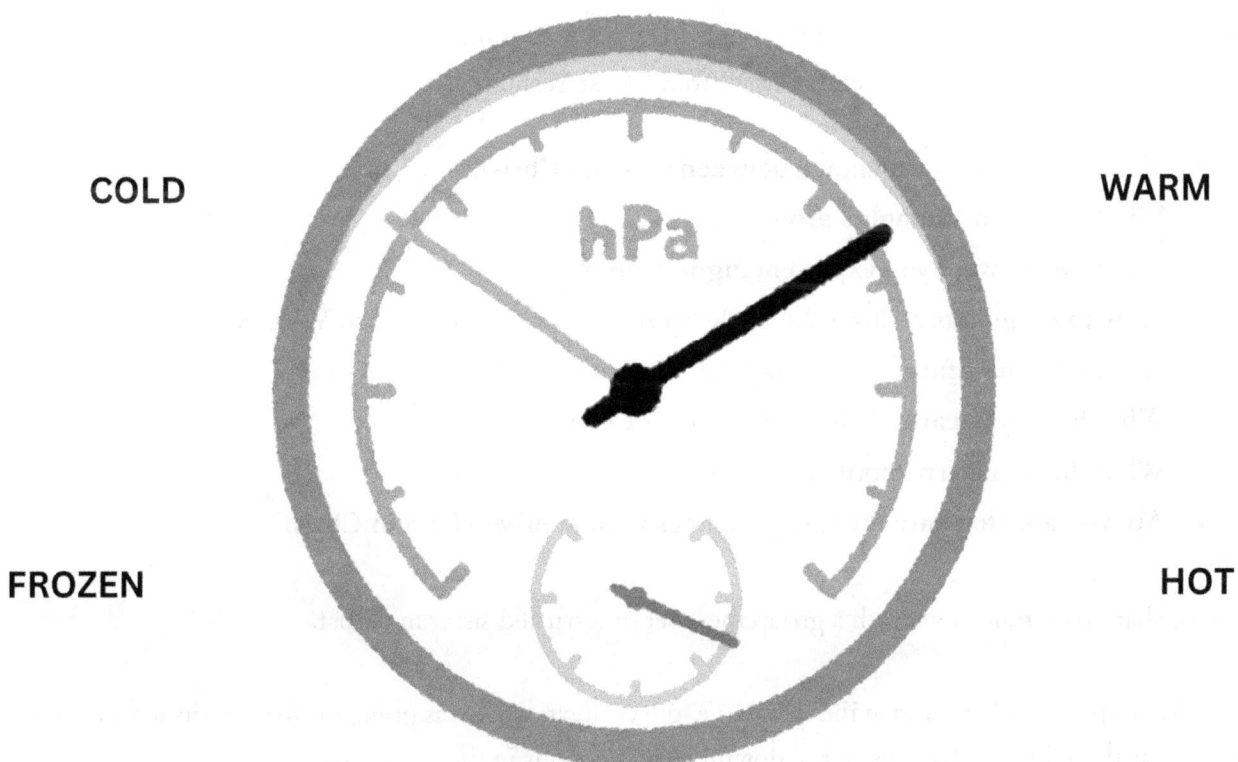

Meditate:

Exercise 3

Prayerfully ask the Holy Spirit to reveal His truth in this next exercise.

- On the barometer above, plot where you discern your relationship with Christ Yeshua to be?
- Ask Yeshua why this is. (Please be prepared to share with others.)
- Have there been any surprises for you when doing this exercise?

Reflect on your thoughts in your personal journal.

Exercise 4

Where Am I?

For this part of the session, we will focus on our relationship with Christ Yeshua (or lack of it). We will explore which parts of our lives we openly invite Christ to be a part of, and which areas we do not.

On your own, prayerfully reflect on the following questions. Take all the time you need. Recall to memory times when you have felt far away from Christ Yeshua.

- **What preceded this distance between you and Christ?**
- **What were your thoughts around this time?**
- **What events were you experiencing in your life?**
- **How (with guidance from the Holy Spirit) have you returned to Yeshua?** **(Please be mindful that you may still be struggling with this.)**
- **What have you learned about the grace of Christ?**
- **What did you learn about yourself?**
- **Are you able to share these experiences with another sister in Christ?**

Now, share your reflections with a group member or a trusted sister in Christ.

Try to be specific when sharing the details, i.e. the context, what was going on for you during this time, and your thoughts and feelings. Write down your reflections in the space provided.

Reflections:

_____

_____

_____

_____

_____

_____

_____

_____

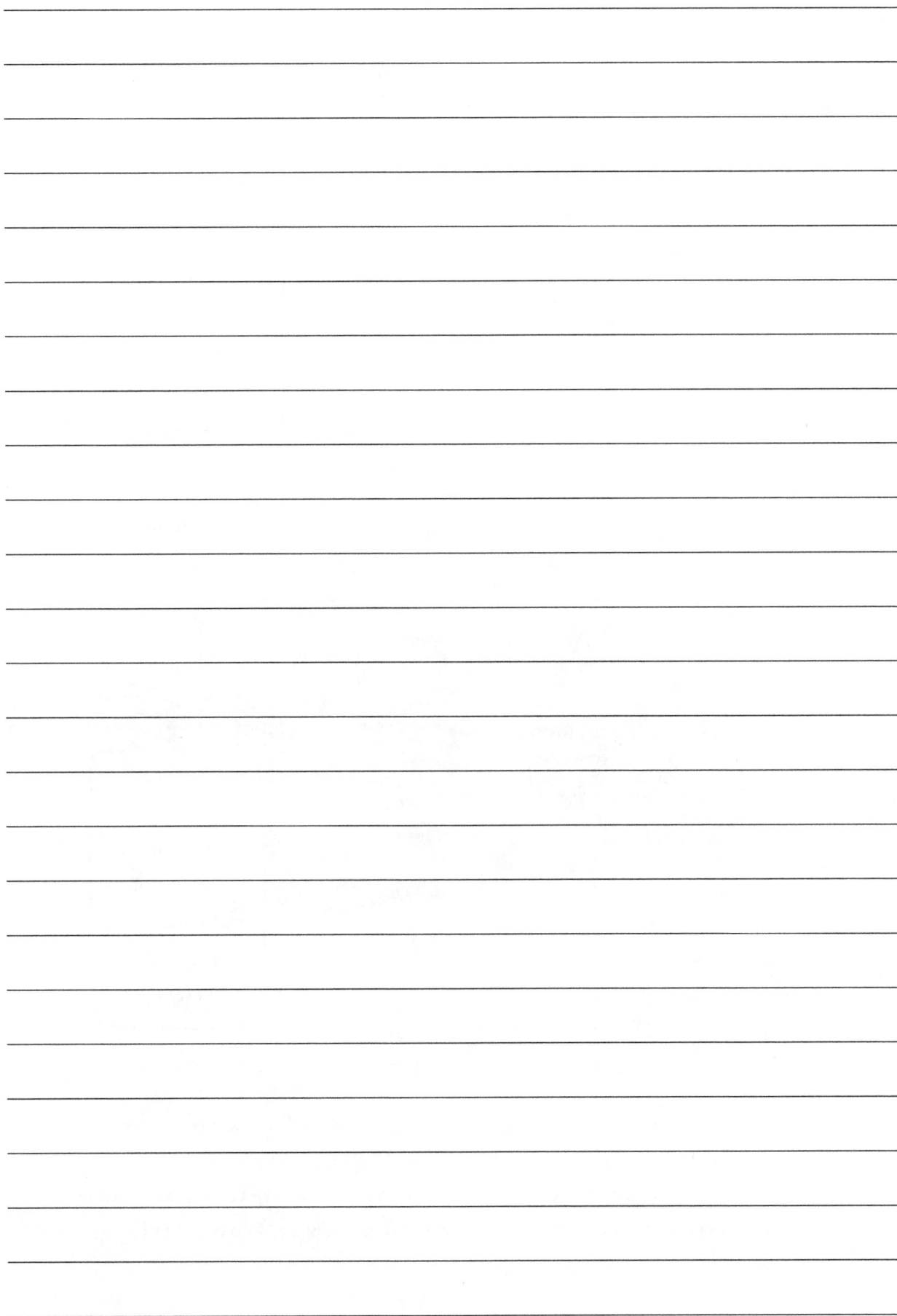

Exercise 5

Using the analogy of an 'open and closed book', in prayer, ask Christ openly and honestly what areas of your life you keep Him away from.

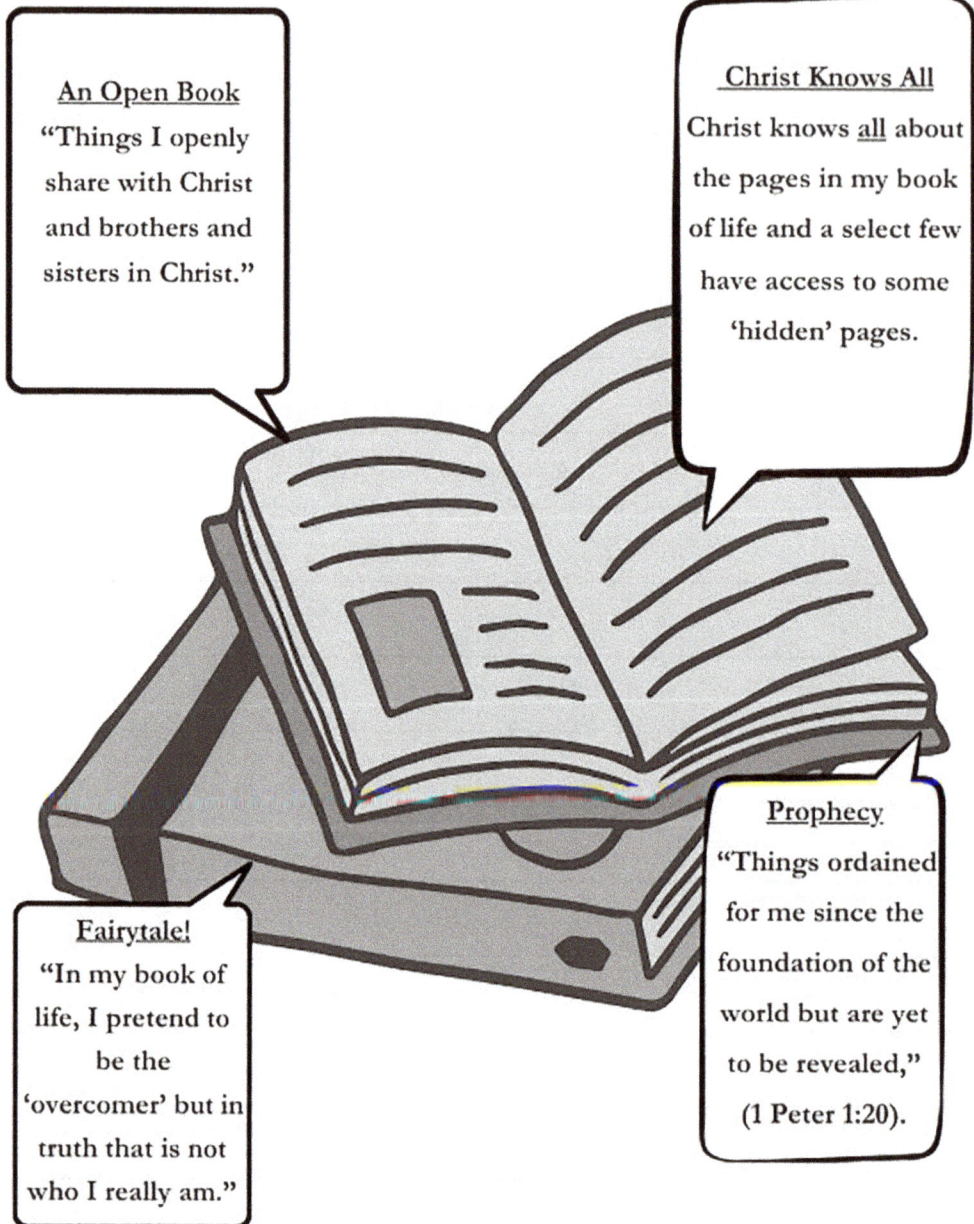

An Open Book
"Things I openly share with Christ and brothers and sisters in Christ."

Christ Knows All
Christ knows all about the pages in my book of life and a select few have access to some 'hidden' pages.

Fairytale!
"In my book of life, I pretend to be the 'overcomer' but in truth that is not who I really am."

Prophecy
"Things ordained for me since the foundation of the world but are yet to be revealed," (1 Peter 1:20).

In James 4:8 (KJV), scripture asks us to
"Draw nigh to God, and he will draw nigh to you."
This is a warning of the outcome of lack of intimacy with
Christ: we fall into sin and move away from Him.

Who is in my House?

Let's dig a little deeper...

We are described in the Bible as spirit, soul, and body (1 Thessalonians 5:23).
Our body houses our soul and spirit. Our soul is where our will, mind, and emotions reside. Our body can be likened to a house; our house or temple (1 Corinthians 6:19) should be a place of safety and intimacy with Yahweh through Christ Yeshua, where we willingly and openly let Christ in.
We should not fear Christ delving into our spirit and soul to help clear the clutter of unhealed pain, unforgiveness, sin, and shame. When wounded, pain begins to clutter our spirit and soul, affecting our intimacy with Christ.

Unforgiveness, sin, and shame can result in physical pain or terminal illness (Hebrew 12:15).
When we seek to keep Christ out of our hurt places and show him only the 'tidy' rooms in our spiritual home, we are in effect saying that we do not want to be intimate with Him. Christ is all-seeing and all-knowing (Matthew 26:20–25). We can keep nothing from Him.

1 Corinthians 6:19 tells us that our body is a temple of the Holy Spirit. In this exercise, we will now use a house as a metaphor for our spirit, soul, and body. The brickwork is our body; the furnishings are our soul; the atmosphere and ambience in our house is our spirit.

Exercise 6: Using the template image of the house on page 14, identify:

- Your favourite room in the house.
- Your special place in the room that you feel safe and secure in.

In pairs, discuss the following:

- What kind of activities do you do in your special room in your home, i.e., sleep, worship, crying, etc.? (These activities may include sinful activities)
- Who can share this special room/space with you, and why?
- What kind of joyful memories do you explore in this room?
- What kind of painful memories do you explore in this room?
- Have you been able to invite Christ into your special place during the most painful times?
- If not, why not?

Continue to prayerfully ask the Holy Spirit for wisdom in completing this exercise.

House Exercise

Use this template to complete Exercise 6 on page 23.

Personal reflections:

_____

_____

_____

_____

_____

_____

_____

_____

_____

_____

_____

_____

_____

_____

_____

_____

_____

_____

_____

_____

_____

_____

_____

Exploring Intimacy

Exercise 7

Think about the word *'intimacy'*. Using the mind map below, jot down as many words you associate with this word. Do not try to censor your words; write down what immediately comes to mind.

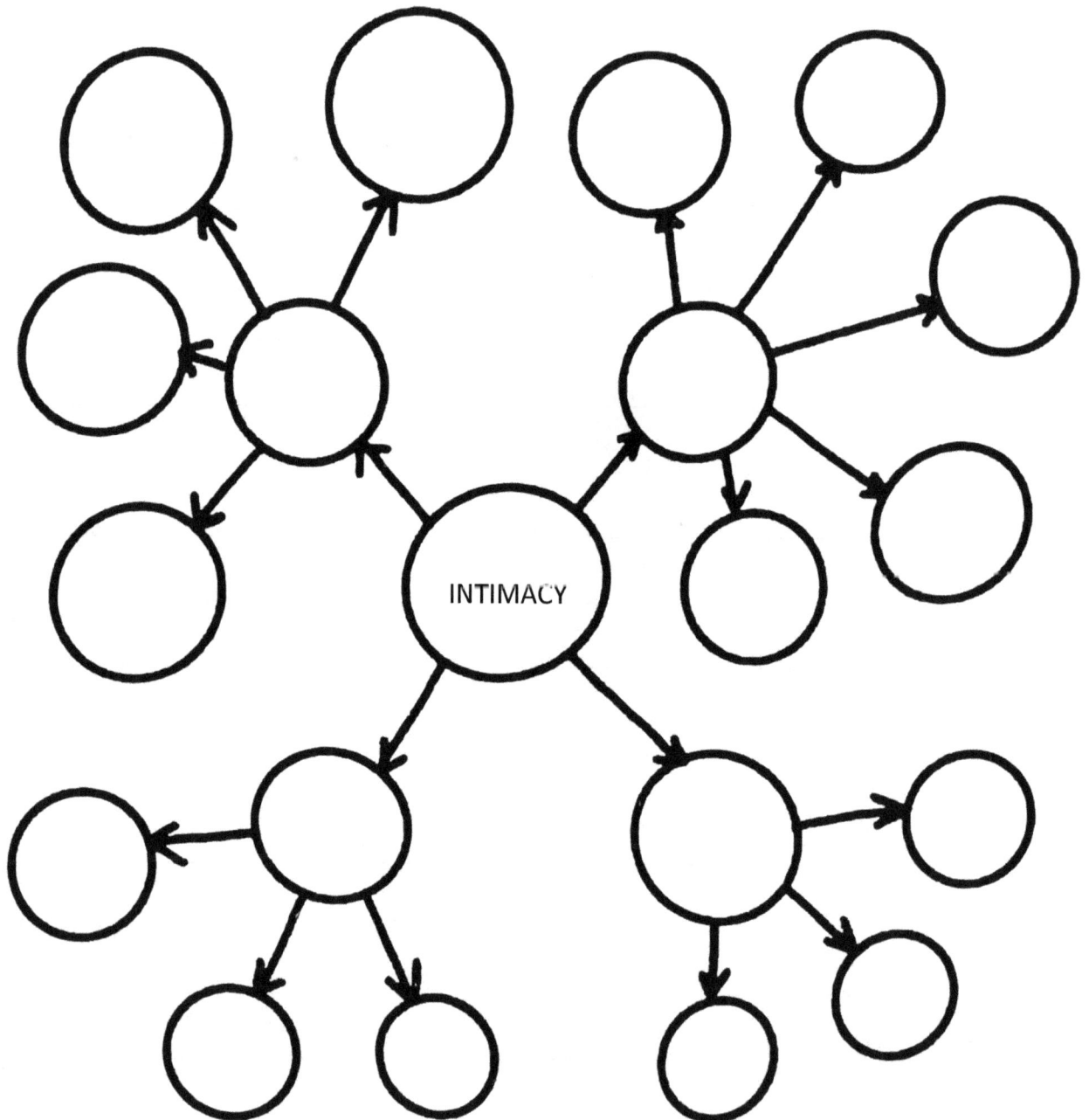

INTIMACY

Exercise 8

"Anyone can be in a relationship, but is every relationship intimate?"

Write down some examples of intimate and non-intimate relationships using the table below.

Intimate Relationships	Non-Intimate Relationships

Exercise 9

Once you have completed the table above, reflect on:

- Your personal experience of intimacy. Reflect on what it means personally for you, and why.
- Has your personal experience of 'intimacy' been a positive or negative experience?
- Think about your earliest experiences of relationships. What did you learn from these relationships? Use the space to write down your reflections.

_____

_____

_____

_____

_____

_____

Exercise 10

Quiet Reflection:

What did I learn about intimacy as a:

- Baby:

....
....
....
....

- Child:

....
....
....
....

- Teenager:

....
....
....
....

- Young Adult:

....
....
....
....

- Adult:

....
....
....
....

Yahweh desired relationship with us...

"For I came down from heaven, not to do mine own will, but the will of him that sent me."
John 6:38 (KJV)

Genesis to Revelation describes a beautiful love story, where Yahweh, through His son Christ Yeshua, desired communion and intimacy with His creation. Genesis 3:8 points to our Father in heaven being relational. Yahweh walked in the garden; He did not talk to Adam and Eve from the clouds of Heaven. After the fall, an emergency restoration plan was needed. The great physician was Christ. Our Father in Heaven sent his son, Christ Yeshua, to earth to communicate fellowship and show us how much Abba Father loves us (John, 3:16, NIV). Yahweh became a man so he could reach us directly.

So, our vinedresser (Yahweh) must have a significant intimate relationship with his vine (Christ) and its branches (us) (John 15:1-11). We are the branches that are attached to the vine. No relationship, no fruit! This is why Christ said that if His branches are not bearing fruit, they will be cut off and thrown in the fire. **What 'fruits' are others witnessing in your life?**

We were made for relationship with Christ

We see an example of the triune relationship between Father, Son, Holy Spirit and man in Genesis 1:26-27 (KJV).

Yahweh declares, *"Let us make man in Our image, according to Our likeness...; let them have dominion over the fish of the sea, over the birds of the air, and over the cattle, over [g]all the earth and over every creeping thing that creeps on the earth.' 27 So God created man in His own image; in the image of God He created him; male and female He created them. 28 Then God blessed them, and God said to them, 'Be fruitful and multiply; fill the earth and subdue it; have dominion over the fish of the sea, over the birds of the air, and over every living thing that [h]moves on the earth."*

The intimate relationships between Father, Son, and Holy Spirit (the Godhead) were what Yahweh desired with His human creation. The great physician intimately designed man and woman in His image. So Yehovah fashioned us in His likeness, knitted us together perfectly, and watched us grow in our mother's womb (Psalm 139:13). How much more intimate is that?

Just as the vine needs to be rooted in the earth, we must be rooted in Yehovah through Christ Yeshua.

Exercise 11

So, reflecting further on your experience of intimacy following these exercises, what have you learnt about your personal experience of intimacy with:

- Christ Yeshua?
- The Holy Spirit?
- Brothers and sisters in Christ?
- Your family?
- Your community?
- Fellow human beings?

Write down any revelations the Holy Spirit has given you.

Please note: If you struggle with being intimate with Christ, how might this affect your ability to be intimate with others?

Yahweh became man...

Christ Yeshua called himself the 'Son of Man' 80 times in the gospels. When Christ calls himself this, there is something that He is trying to communicate to us. Christ is communicating his relationship and connection with the Kingdom of God and His connection with man and woman.

We must **not** forget that:

- Christ became a man to reconcile the relationship between man and Yahweh (Hebrews 2:12-18).
- Christ came to earth and was born of a woman (Galatians 4:4).
- Christ grew like other humans (Luke 2:40).
- Christ lived as a man until he ascended into heaven (Acts 1:9).
- Christ experienced human emotions. Christ was compassionate (Luke 19:41-44).
- Christ **will** come again (Hebrews 9:28).

Developing intimacy with Abba Father?

On page 9, I asked where you would plot your relationship with Christ on the barometer. This is now the opportunity to make things right with Yahweh. Like the prodigal son in Luke 15:11-32, He wants us to return to Him. Use the template to keep revisiting this exercise as you work through this workbook.

It is important to note that if you are struggling to be in relationship with Christ, you are struggling with Abba Father and the Holy Spirit. Remember when Christ Yeshua said, **'he that hath seen me hath seen the Father; and how sayest thou then, Shew us the Father?'** (John 14:9 KJV). Father, Son, and Holy Spirit cannot be separated; they are one; they are triune.

So, ask yourself, **'Do I want an intimate relationship with the Triune God?'** If the answer is **'Yes'**, then the Holy Spirit (the Spirit of Truth) is waiting to lead you back to Christ.

If not, put this workbook down and spend time fasting and praying for revelation.

How can we develop intimacy with Abba Father?

- **Repent** (from your heart) all known and unknown sins. (Unknown sin may be in relation to your ancestors who may have rejected Christ.)

- **Repent** for not drawing near to Christ (John 1:1).

- **Declare** Christ Yeshua as your Lord and Saviour so we may be reconciled to Abba Father (2 Peter 3:9).

- **Forgive** those who may have contributed to your falling away, but remember, Yahweh gave us **all** free will, so we need to take responsibility for our actions. Remember, Christ said, 'Be ye angry, and sin not.' (Ephesians 4:26 KJV)

- **Reconcile** (if possible, and if safe to do so) with those you have forgiven. The Bible says that when Yahweh forgives you, He remembers your sin no more. You must do likewise (Hebrews 8:12).

- **Ask Yahweh to forgive you** – The Bible says if we confess our sins, Yahweh will forgive us (1 John 1:9).

- **Spend time daily in His Word.** Isaiah 55:6 KJV says, **'Seek ye the Lord while he may be found, call ye upon him while he is near.'** In our daily intimate conversations with Abba Father, listen to what He has to say to you.

- **When we draw close to Abba Father, He will draw close to us** (James 4:8). In truly being intimate with Abba Father, we will fulfil Christ's greatest commandment, found in Matthew 22:37-40.

Benefits of My Relationship with Christ Yeshua

Write down how you have and will benefit from an intimate relationship with Christ. You can use the 'notes' section at the back of the book to add more. Use the Bible to help you in your study.

Exercise 12

1. ....
2. ....
3. ....
4. ....
5. ....
6. ....
7. ....
8. ....
9. ....
10. ....
11. ....
12. ....
13. ....
14. ....
15. ....
16. ....
17. ....
18. ....
19. ....
20. ....
21. ....
22. ....
23. ....
24. ....

Continue with a separate sheet.

How can you begin to develop intimacy with Abba Father through Christ Yeshua? List your thoughts and reflections below.

_____

_____

_____

_____

_____

_____

_____

_____

_____

_____

_____

_____

_____

_____

_____

_____

_____

_____

_____

_____

Bringing it all together

- When in a healthy relationship with someone we care about, we are happy to listen to what they say and not to take offence because we know they only want the best for us. Abba Father has wanted the best for us since creation. He provided for Adam and Eve in the Garden of Eden, even after they rejected Him! Christ changed all of this when He declared on the cross... **"It is finished!"** (John 19:30 KJV).

- When we are intimate with Christ Yeshua, it means that we are open to what Yahweh has to say to us. Christ is our intercessor. **No relationship with Christ, no relationship with Yahweh and The Holy Spirit!** More often, our distance from the Godhead results from our not wanting to listen or act when Abba Father speaks to us through His Holy Spirit. Abba Father loves His children, and it is not His desire that any should perish (2 Peter 3:9).

- Revisit the scripture about your connection to the true vine, Christ Yeshua. We know that any branch that does not bear fruit is cut off and thrown into the fire (John 15:2). Therefore, a distinct part of being intimate with Abba Father means that you should be prepared to be pruned, tended to, and cared for, no matter how difficult this might be.

- Yahweh's pruning is necessary. Think about some of the pruning the Lord has done in your life. **What has He cut away, or who has He cut away, and why do you think this was? What still needs to be cut away?** You can use the notes page to write your thoughts and reflections.

Learning Reflection:

Exercise 13

- What did I learn about my relationship with Christ in this chapter?

....

....

....

....

....

- What are my action points?

....

....

....

....

....

- To whom am I accountable when working through these action points?

....

....

....

....

....

Reflections:

Call To Action

Dear Sister,

If you have managed to complete this chapter, well done. I can assure you that Christ is beginning His work in you and will see it through to its completion (Philippians 1:6). Amen!

You may not yet be a believer in Christ and have come across this book by divine appointment. You may be new to Christianity and Christ is calling you to be a member of His worldwide family. You may be completing this workbook alone, or you may have been invited to join a Christian women's group to complete this workbook together. Whatever the reason, Christ wants to save you and redeem you from hell and eternity without Him.

Maybe you are already a professed Christian, but your Christian Walk has gone cold or is lukewarm. Remember what scripture says about the lukewarm Christian? *'I will spue you out.'* (Revelation 3:16 KJV)

If this describes you, it is not too late to invite/reinvite Christ Yeshua into your heart. To make Him your Lord and Saviour.

How might you do this, you ask

Take your time and in a quiet space:

- Repent (express sincere regret or remorse about the sinful way you have lived).
- Ask Christ to forgive you and save you from the rightful penalty of eternal death (which you rightfully deserve).
- Confess with your mouth that Christ is Lord, 'and believe with your heart that Yahweh raised Christ Yeshua from the dead'. (Romans 10:9)
- If you willingly surrender and say this prayer, asking Christ Yeshua into your heart, spirit, soul, and mind, scripture says, 'You will be saved!'

There is some amazing news I want to share with you once you have decided to be a follower of Christ Yeshua. Luke 15:10 says, **"Likewise, I say unto you, there is joy in the presence of the angels of God over one sinner that repenteth."**

Sister in Christ, Heaven is rejoicing!

Homework 1

Spend time with Christ Yeshua in prayer and conversation. Complete your 500-word/picture/collage reflection. Reflect on some of the questions in this workbook in your personal journal.

What have you personally learnt about your relationship and intimacy with:

- Abba Father?
- Christ Yeshua?
- The Holy Spirit?
- With yourself?
- With others?

END OF MODULE 1

Philippians 4:13 (KJV)

"I can do all things through Christ which strengtheneth me."

MODULE 2
SELF-ESTEEM &
SELF-WORTH

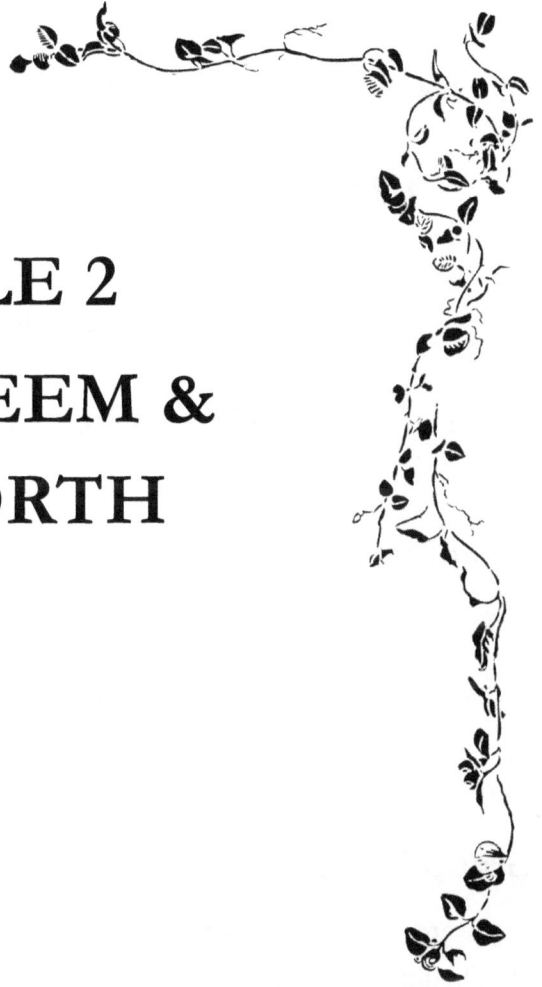

Module 2: Self Esteem & Self-Worth

**"He hath sent me to bind up the brokenhearted,
to proclaim liberty to the captives,
and the opening of the prison to them that are bound"**

Isaiah 61:1 (KJV)

Opening Prayer:

Group Contract:

If you are completing this programme within a group, please remind participants of the importance of adhering to and remaining committed to the group contract. Revisit the contract at the start of each session to ensure the group's safety. The group must adhere to it.

Module 1 Reflection

If working as a group, set aside 15-30 minutes to share your reflections from Module 1.
Please keep to time boundaries.

Module Aims:

Explore personal meanings of value and esteem as a daughter in Christ.

Module Outcomes:

By the end of the session, delegates will be able to:

- Differentiate between God's value of a woman and how the world values a woman.
- Recognise how you value yourself and the challenges with this.
- Identify how your value is related to self-esteem.

Session 2: This week we will be exploring - Self Esteem & Self Worth.

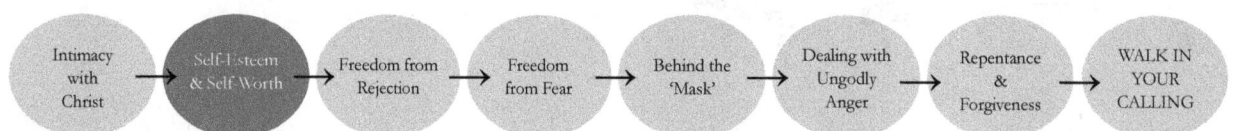

Intimacy with Christ → Self-Esteem & Self-Worth → Freedom from Rejection → Freedom from Fear → Behind the 'Mask' → Dealing with Ungodly Anger → Repentance & Forgiveness → WALK IN YOUR CALLING

A Message to My Daughter

Proverbs 3:15-18 (KJV)

"15 She is more precious than rubies:

and all the things thou canst desire

are not to be compared unto her.

16 Length of days is in her right hand;

and in her left hand riches and honour.

17 Her ways are ways of pleasantness,

and all her paths are peace.

18 She is a tree of life to them that lay hold upon her:

and happy is everyone that retaineth her."

Exploring Our Worth Through God's Word...

Exercise 1

Reflection

Take a moment to reflect on the piece of scripture on page 33.

Reflect on the following questions:

- Do you feel this way about yourself? If not, why?
- Reflect on the areas of your life that you exhibit this way of being.
- **Share your reflections with Christ Yeshua, a sister in Christ, or your group.**

Self-Worth and Women:

The word 'self-esteem' is a term used in psychology. It is a way a person measures their worth and the regard they have for themselves.

The world view also believes that how you think about yourself will affect what you believe, your mindset, and how you will live your life. Proverbs 23:7 makes it clear that our thoughts are powerful and can plot our destiny for good or evil.

Solomon in his wisdom wrote this proverb even before psychology existed.

The Bible shows us how parents can help or hinder us from having the proper basis of self-esteem by how they raised us, but Yahweh has ultimately given us responsibility for how we respond.

Exercise 2

What is meant by 'value'?

(10-minute group discussion/personal reflection)

_____

_____

_____

_____

Exercise 2

GROUP DISCUSSION

What are some of the things you value in your life and why?

- **Write your reflections here:**

....

....

....

....

....

....

....

....

....

VALUE =
My Net Worth?

Exercise 3

In pairs discuss...

1. How does the world measure a person's worth?

2. How do you measure your worth and value?

3. How does Yahweh measure your worth?

4. Write down three Bible scriptures where Yahweh speaks of your value.

5. Do you truly believe in what Abba Father says about you? If not, why not?

Reflections

_____

_____

_____

_____

_____

_____

_____

_____

_____

_____

_____

_____

_____

Food for Thought...

Is your 'worth' the total of your investments, money, house, job title, and possessions? Worldly self-worth is measured in the following way:

- who you are surrounded by,
- what you do,
- how much money you have,
- what you have achieved,
- how you look,
- if you feel good about who you are.

For many, self-esteem is adversely affected because they may have been made redundant, lost their home, or they may have had to sell their possessions. Some people may even tie their worth to their title, career, salary, marital status, and how many 'likes' they receive on social media platforms.

Christ taught us that our life doesn't consist of the things that we possess on earth (Luke 12:15).

Value of a Human

The UK government in England and Wales has estimated a child's or adult's life to be around the minute figure of approximately £20K. According to the UK government, this is what a family would be compensated if someone we loved was harmed or died due to negligence. **What is the figure your government has associated with your human value in the part of the world where you live?**

This amount feels very pitiful, as Yahweh makes it clear how precious we are in 1 Peter 2:9 (KJV), *'But ye are a chosen generation, a royal priesthood, an holy nation, a peculiar people; that ye should shew forth the praises of him who hath called you out of darkness into his marvellous light.'*

What if God calculated your worth in this way? What would it mean for you?

Reflections

....

....

....

....

NOW...

Let's look at how Abba Father values your life.

> *'But God commendeth his love toward us, in that, while we were yet sinners,*
> *Christ died for us.'*
> Romans 5:8, New King James (KJV)

- What does this tell you about how Abba Father values your life? Take a moment to really think about this. Yahweh allowed His son to be the ultimate sacrifice for YOU.
- What does this mean for you knowing this?

SELF-ESTEEM

- King Solomon, in approximately 717 BC, made it clear that how we think about ourselves will affect what we believe, our mindset, and how we live our lives. The world has tried to reinvent this instruction and make it its own. However, a 'world view' can change from day to day, but the Word of God does not (Proverbs 23:7)!

- The Bible teaches us to trust and believe in Christ Yeshua, as He is the source of life!

- He also warns us that our earthly parents can help or hinder children from having the proper basis of self-esteem by how they raised us (Proverbs 22:6) and that Yahweh gives His children the responsibility to choose.

Exercise 4

ON A SCALE OF 1-10,
(1 = Poor - 10 = Excellent)
Where would you plot your self-esteem?
In pairs, discuss the reasons for your
answer and write your reflections below.

Write your number here ( ) and reflect on your reasons for this:
(Please note: if you rate yourself highly on the scale, this should be evident in your life.)

....

....

....

....

....

....

Exploring Childhood

God's instruction to parents:

Proverbs 22:6 (KJV), 'Train up a child in the way he should go: and when he is old, he will not depart from it.'

Proverbs 13:24 (KJV), 'He that spareth his rod hateth his son: but he that loveth him chasteneth him betimes.'

As parents/caregivers, we must pay attention to the following scripture...

Ephesians 6:4 (KJV), 'And, ye fathers, provoke not your children to wrath: but bring them up in the nurture and admonition of the Lord.'

Exercise 5

Group Discussion

Please share only what you feel able to share.

- How was the Lord guiding your parents/caregivers when raising you?
- Did your parent's pay attention to the Bible in this respect?
- How did you view your parents? Were they:
  - Fair, loving and boundaried parents/caregivers, etc? or,
  - Unfair, unloving, disrespectful of your boundaries?
  - Violent and dismissive?
  - Lacking responsibility?
  - **Any other reflections?**

"I must be approved by others"

Exercise 6

On your own... (two minutes)

Take two minutes to prayerfully ask God to reveal His truth about the images on page 40 and the questions below.

In pairs/on your own... (eight minutes)

- Briefly discuss/explore which images resonate with how you were raised.
- Explore how a parent(s) can impact the way we value ourselves.
- Explore how your parent(s) influenced how **you** value yourself.
- Name and describe the behaviours you exhibit to demonstrate how you value yourself.
- How might these experiences distort/enhance the way you think Yahweh sees you?
- Name and describe the behaviours you exhibit to demonstrate how you **do not** value yourself.

Notes:

_____

_____

_____

_____

_____

_____

_____

_____

_____

How Precious We Are To Abba Father...

Below are **just** 21 Bible Verses about how precious we are to Abba Father. We are so precious. He sent his only begotten son to die for us so that we may live. As children with earthly parents, we may not understand this; as adults, we may still struggle to understand what Abba Father sees in us. We may feel unworthy, unloved, and rejected, but we realise how priceless we are when we see ourselves through Christ's eyes. These truths are part of the 'Armour of God' (Ephesians 6:10-18). These truths deliver us from the bondage of sin; Christ came to earth out of his great love for us.

It can be difficult to comprehend Yahweh's love for us fully, but as we draw near to Him, we discover how wonderfully overwhelming His love is. The Bible says that Yahweh so loved the world that He allowed His only begotten Son to be led as a lamb to slaughter (John 3:16). Christ loved His Father so much that He shed His blood for us, even when we were sinners in His eyes.

When we can genuinely believe the truth, we can begin to act like the loved child we are and were always meant to be.

Exercise 7

To understand how valuable we are to Yahweh, read the verses on pages 42–44.
Reflect on:

- **Which of the verses stood out for you?**
- **Why are these verses so meaningful for you?**
- **Mediate on your chosen verses and ask the Holy Spirit to reveal what the Lord wants you to know and believe about how He sees you.**

Then, share your scripture verses with another group member or a sister in Christ.

Scripture Verses

1. **John 3:16 (KJV):** For God so loved the world, that He gave his only begotten Son, that whosoever believeth in Him should not perish, but have everlasting life.

2. **John 3:16 (KJV):** For God so loved the world, that He gave his only begotten Son, that whosoever believeth in Him should not perish, but have everlasting life.

3. **Romans 5:8 (KJV):** But God commendeth His love toward us, in that, while we were yet sinners, Christ died for us.

4. **Ephesians 1:4 (KJV):** According as he hath chosen us in Him before the foundation of the world, that we should be holy and without blame before Him in love.

5. **Psalm 139:14 (KJV):** I will praise thee; for I am fearfully and wonderfully made: marvellous are thy works; and that my soul knoweth right well.

6. **Psalm 107:43 (KJV):** Who so is wise, and will observe these things, even they shall understand the loving kindness of the Lord.

7. **John 1:12 (KJV):** But as many as received Him, to them gave He power to become the sons of God, even to them that believe on His name.

8. **Zephaniah 3:17 (KJV):** The Lord thy God in the midst of thee is mighty; He will save, He will rejoice over thee with joy; He will rest in His love, He will joy over thee with singing.

9. **Deuteronomy 7:9 (KJV):** Know therefore that the Lord thy God, He is God, the faithful God, which keepeth covenant and mercy with them that love Him and keep His commandments to a thousand generations.

10. **Psalm 136:26 (KJV):** O give thanks unto the God of heaven: for His mercy endureth for ever.

11. **Psalm 86:15 (KJV):** But thou, O Lord, art a God full of compassion, and gracious, long suffering, and plenteous in mercy and truth.

12. **John 15:13 (KJV):** Greater love hath no man than this, that a man lay down his life for his friends.

13. **Romans 6:23 (KJV):** For the wages of sin is death; but the gift of God is eternal life through Jesus Christ our Lord.

14. **Jeremiah 29:11 (KJV):** For I know the thoughts that I think toward you, saith the Lord, thoughts of peace, and not of evil, to give you an expected end.

15. **1 John 4:4 (KJV):** Ye are of God, little children, and have overcome them: because greater is He that is in you, than He that is in the world.

16. **Ephesians 2:10 (KJV):** For we are His workmanship, created in Christ Jesus unto good works, which God hath before ordained that we should walk in them.

17. **Romans 8:17 (KJV):** And if children, then heirs; heirs of God, and joint heirs with Christ; if so be that we suffer with Him, that we may be also glorified together.

18. **Romans 5:10 (KJV):** For if, when we were enemies, we were reconciled to God by the death of His Son, much more, being reconciled, we shall be saved by His life.

19. **John 10:10 (KJV):** The thief cometh not, but for to steal, and to kill, and to destroy. I am come that they might have life, and that they might have it more abundantly.

20. **1 John 4:16 (KJV):** And we have known and believed the love that God hath to us. God is love; and he that dwelleth in love dwelleth in God, and God in him.

21. **2 Corinthians 5:21 (KJV):** For He hath made Him to be sin for us, who knew no sin; that we might be made the righteousness of God in Him.

Q. Can you think of more verses demonstrating Yahweh's love for His children? Write them down in your notebook.

How Precious Are You To Abba Father?

I have used the diamond analogy to demonstrate how precious you are to Abba Father. Often, we do not believe that we are precious in the sight of Yahweh. This may be because we are not used to hearing kind words spoken over us by Yahweh or by others. His words are words of affirmation, love, correction, etc.; they build us up, and they do not tear us down.

It is estimated that there are over 160 'Identity in Christ' verses in the Bible. This is amazing! The Holy Spirit speaks loving affirmations over us daily. That is why it is so important that we spend time in His Word! Yet we often default to the self-curses and harsh words that were spoken over us to create and shape our identity.

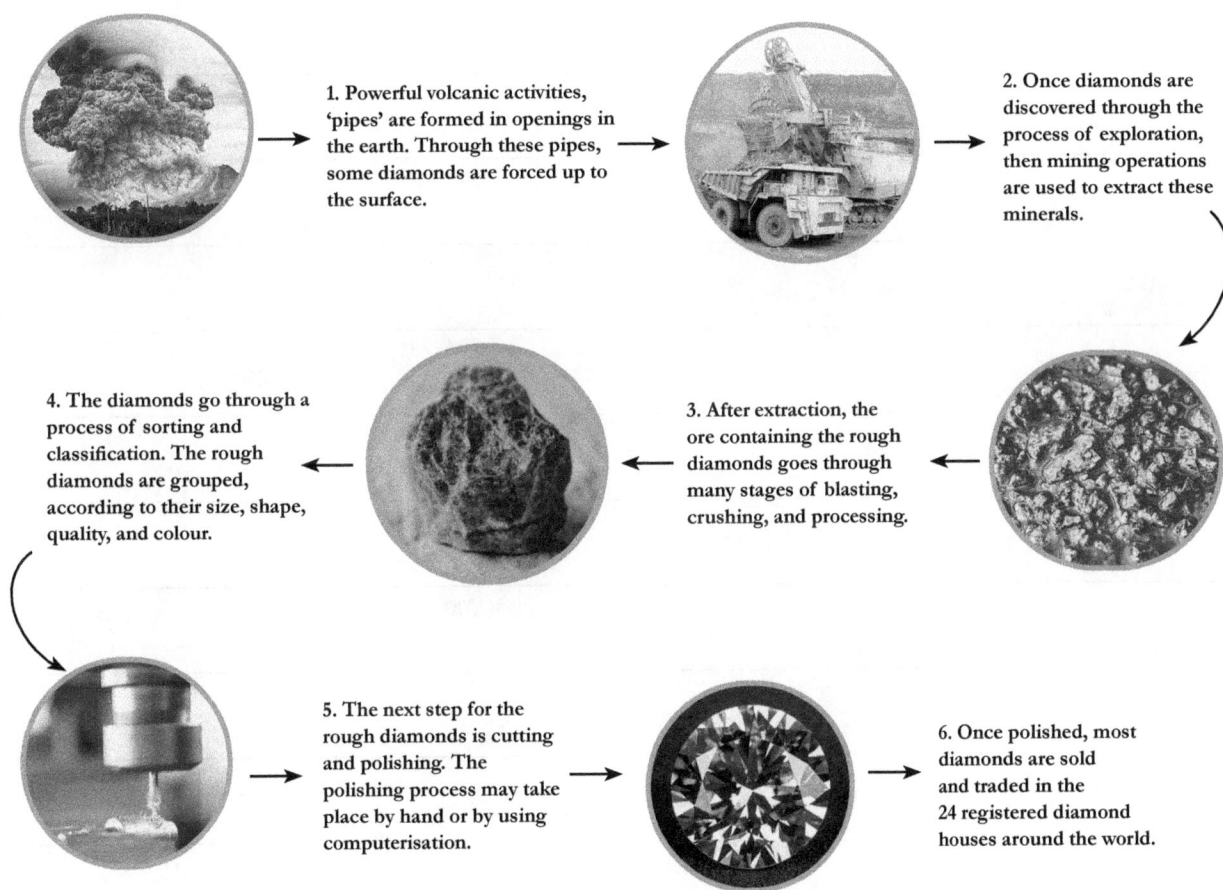

1. Powerful volcanic activities, 'pipes' are formed in openings in the earth. Through these pipes, some diamonds are forced up to the surface.

2. Once diamonds are discovered through the process of exploration, then mining operations are used to extract these minerals.

3. After extraction, the ore containing the rough diamonds goes through many stages of blasting, crushing, and processing.

4. The diamonds go through a process of sorting and classification. The rough diamonds are grouped, according to their size, shape, quality, and colour.

5. The next step for the rough diamonds is cutting and polishing. The polishing process may take place by hand or by using computerisation.

6. Once polished, most diamonds are sold and traded in the 24 registered diamond houses around the world.

This short example should demonstrate how Yahweh is seeking us and refining us to shine like the 'diamond' we were created to be.

Reflections:

Call to Action

Dear Sister,

If you have managed to complete this chapter, well done. I can assure you that Christ is beginning His work in you and will see it through to its completion (Philippians 1:6). Amen!

You may not yet be a believer in Christ and have come across this book by divine appointment. You may be new to Christianity, and Christ is calling you to be a member of His worldwide family. You may be completing this workbook alone, or you may have been invited to join a Christian women's group to complete this workbook together. Whatever the reason, Christ wants to save you and redeem you from hell and eternity without Him.

Maybe you are already a professed Christian, but your Christian Walk has gone cold or is lukewarm. Remember what scripture says about the lukewarm Christian? *"I will spue out of my mouth"* (Revelation 3:16 KJV).

If this describes you, it is not too late to invite/reinvite Christ Yeshua into your heart, to make Him your Lord and Saviour.

How might you do this?

Take your time and in a quiet space:

- Repent (express sincere regret or remorse about the sinful way you have lived).
- Ask Christ to forgive you and save you from the rightful penalty of eternal death (which you rightfully deserve).
- Confess with your mouth that Christ is Lord, 'and believe with your heart that Yahweh raised Christ Yeshua from the dead' (Romans 10:9).
- If you willingly surrender and say this prayer, asking Christ Yeshua into your heart, spirit, soul, and mind, scripture says, 'You will be saved!'

There is some amazing news I want to share with you once you have decided to be a follower of Christ Yeshua. Luke 15:10 says, **"Likewise, I say unto you, there is joy in the presence of the angels of God over one sinner that repenteth."**

Sister in Christ, Heaven is rejoicing!

Homework 2

Prayerfully spend time and reflect on the women of Yahweh in the Bible. Allow the Holy Spirit to lead you to choose one woman from the list of women below. Read the Bible story surrounding their character, their journey, and Yahweh's purpose for their life. Reflect on how the Bible speaks of this woman's relationship with the Godhead. Reflect on her significance and purpose in Abba's plan for humanity.

Then, in your journal, reflect on the following questions prayerfully:

- Why did you choose this woman of God?
- How does the Bible talk about their value?
- What is God trying to show you about the value of this woman?
- How is Yahweh trying to communicate in His Word how you are valued as a woman of God?
- Write your reflections on your notes page.
- Prepare a five-minute timed presentation titled: **How this Woman of God Reflects my life.**
- Be prepared to present in your next session. If you are completing this alone, please share your presentation with a trusted sister in Christ.

POWERFUL WOMEN OF GOD

1. Eve: first woman created by Yah
2. Sarah: mother of the Jewish nation
3. Rebekah: intervening wife of Isaac
4. Rachel: wife of Jacob and mother of Joseph
5. Leah: wife of Jacob through deceit
6. Jochebed: mother of Moses
7. Miriam: sister of Moses
8. Rahab: unlikely ancestor of Jesus
9. Deborah: influential female judge
10. Ruth: virtuous ancestor of Yeshua
11. Hannah: mother of Samuel
12. Bathsheba: mother of Solomon
13. Esther: influential Persian Queen
14. Mary: obedient mother of Yeshua
15. Elizabeth: mother of John the Baptist
16. Martha: anxious sister of Lazarus
17. Mary of Bethany: loving follower of Jesus
18. Mary Magdalene: unwavering disciple of Yeshua

Reflections:

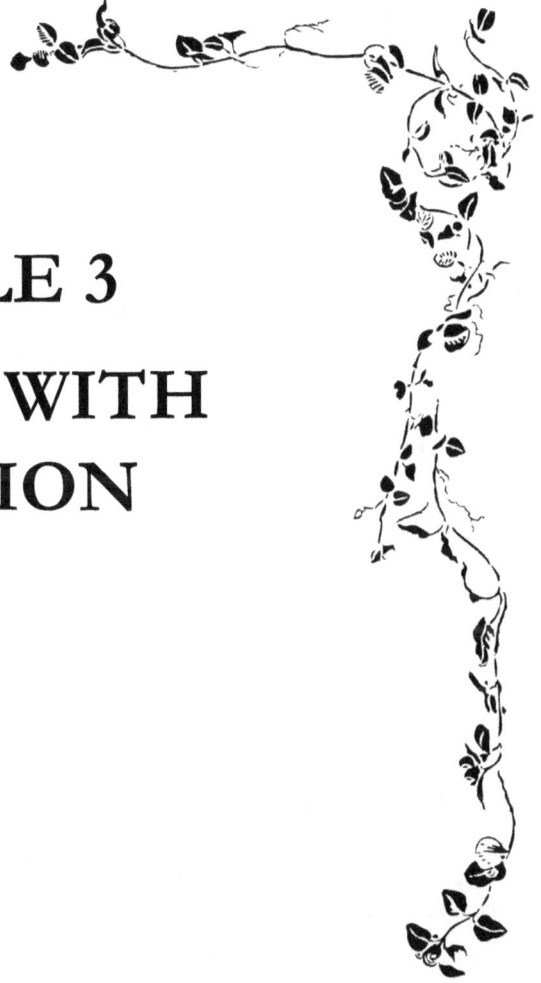

MODULE 3

DEALING WITH REJECTION

Module 3: Dealing With Rejection

"When my father and mother
forsake me,
then the Lord will take me up."
Psalm 27:10 (KJV)

Opening Prayer:

Group Contract:

If you are completing this programme within a group, I would strongly advise that you remind participants of the importance of adhering to and remaining committed to the group contract. Revisit the contract at the start of each session to ensure the safety of the group. It is important that the group adhere to it.

Module 2 Reflection:

If working as group, set aside 15-30 minutes to share your *'Women of God'* personal reflections from Module 2. Once everyone has presented, spend five minutes discussing your learning. Please keep to time boundaries.

Module Aims:

Explore personal meanings of rejection as a daughter in Christ and how rejection has affected and continues to affect your life.

Give a 5-minute presentation on your chosen woman in the bible.

Module Outcomes:

By the end of the session, delegates will be able to:

- Name three significant experiences of personal rejection.
- Describe the ways in which rejection from others has affected and influenced your life.
- Determine the ways in which your personal experience of rejection is preventing you from fully accepting Christ's acceptance of you.

Module 3: We will be exploring - 'Rejection'.

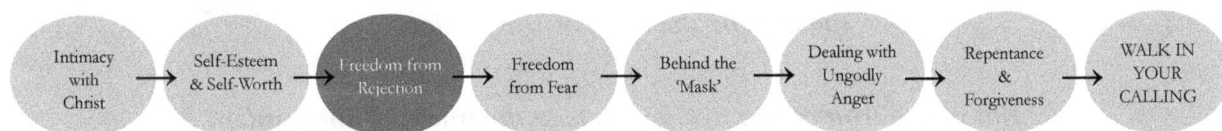

Intimacy with Christ → Self-Esteem & Self-Worth → Freedom from Rejection → Freedom from Fear → Behind the 'Mask' → Dealing with Ungodly Anger → Repentance & Forgiveness → WALK IN YOUR CALLING

Bible Reading

Genesis 3:1-24 (KJV)

'3 Now the serpent was more subtle than any beast of the field
which the Lord God had made. And he said unto the woman,
Yea, hath God said, Ye shall not eat of every tree of the garden?

[2] And the woman said unto the serpent, We may eat of
the fruit of the trees of the garden:

[3] But of the fruit of the tree which is in the midst of the garden,
God hath said, Ye shall not eat of it, neither shall ye touch it, lest ye die.

[4] And the serpent said unto the woman, Ye shall not surely die:

[5] For God doth know that in the day ye eat thereof, then your eyes
shall be opened, and ye shall be as gods, knowing good and evil.

[6] And when the woman saw that the tree was good for food,
and that it was pleasant to the eyes, and a tree to be desired to make
one wise, she took of the fruit thereof, and did eat, and gave
also unto her husband with her; and he did eat.

[7] And the eyes of them both were opened, and they knew
that they were naked; and they sewed fig leaves
together and made themselves aprons.

[8] And they heard the voice of the Lord God walking in the
garden in the cool of the day: and Adam and his wife hid
themselves from the presence of the Lord God
amongst the trees of the garden.

[9] And the Lord God called unto Adam,
and said unto him, Where art thou?

[10] And he said, I heard thy voice in the garden, and
I was afraid, because I was naked; and I hid myself.

*¹¹ And he said, Who told thee that thou wast naked? Hast thou eaten of
the tree, whereof I commanded thee that thou shouldest not eat?*

*¹² And the man said, The woman whom thou gavest to be with me,
she gave me of the tree, and I did eat.*

*¹³ And the Lord God said unto the woman, What is this that thou hast done?
And the woman said, The serpent beguiled me, and I did eat.*

*¹⁴ And the Lord God said unto the serpent, Because thou hast done this,
thou art cursed above all cattle, and above every beast of the field; upon thy
belly shalt thou go, and dust shalt thou eat all the days of thy life:*

*¹⁵ And I will put enmity between thee and the woman, and between
thy seed and her seed; it shall bruise thy head, and thou shalt bruise his heel.*

*¹⁶ Unto the woman he said, I will greatly multiply thy sorrow and thy conception;
in sorrow thou shalt bring forth children; and thy desire shall be to
thy husband, and he shall rule over thee.*

*¹⁷ And unto Adam he said, Because thou hast hearkened unto the voice
of thy wife, and hast eaten of the tree, of which I commanded thee, saying,
Thou shalt not eat of it: cursed is the ground for thy sake;
in sorrow shalt thou eat of it all the days of thy life;*

*¹⁸ Thorns also and thistles shall it bring forth to thee;
and thou shalt eat the herb of the field;*

*¹⁹ In the sweat of thy face shalt thou eat bread, till thou return
unto the ground; for out of it wast thou taken: for dust thou art,
and unto dust shalt thou return.*

²⁰ And Adam called his wife's name Eve; because she was the mother of all living.

*²¹ Unto Adam also and to his wife did the Lord God make coats
of skins, and clothed them.*

*²² And the Lord God said, Behold, the man is become as one of us,
to know good and evil: and now, lest he put forth his hand,
and take also of the tree of life, and eat, and live for ever:*

*²³ Therefore the Lord God sent him forth from the garden of Eden,
to till the ground from whence he was taken.*

*²⁴ So he drove out the man; and he placed at the east of the garden
of Eden Cherubims, and a flaming sword which turned every way, to
keep the way of the tree of life."*

Exercise 1

Bible Reflections:

- How does this chapter in scripture talk about the nature of rejection?
- Reflect on the consequences of Eve's actions.
- Discuss the consequences of 'the fall' in society today.
- How does this scripture demonstrate Adam and Eve's rejection of Abba Father?

Reflections:

_____

_____

_____

_____

_____

_____

_____

_____

_____

_____

_____

_____

Exercise 2

Exploring Rejection...

So, thinking about the word 'rejection', jot down as many words you associate with this word using the mind map below. Do not try to censor your words; write down what immediately comes to mind.

Once you have completed the mind map, reflect on:

- What thoughts and feelings would you associate with the word 'rejection'?
- Your personal experience of rejection. Consider what it means personally for you and why.
- Has it been a positive or negative experience?
- **Share your mind map in pairs or with a trusted sister in Christ.**

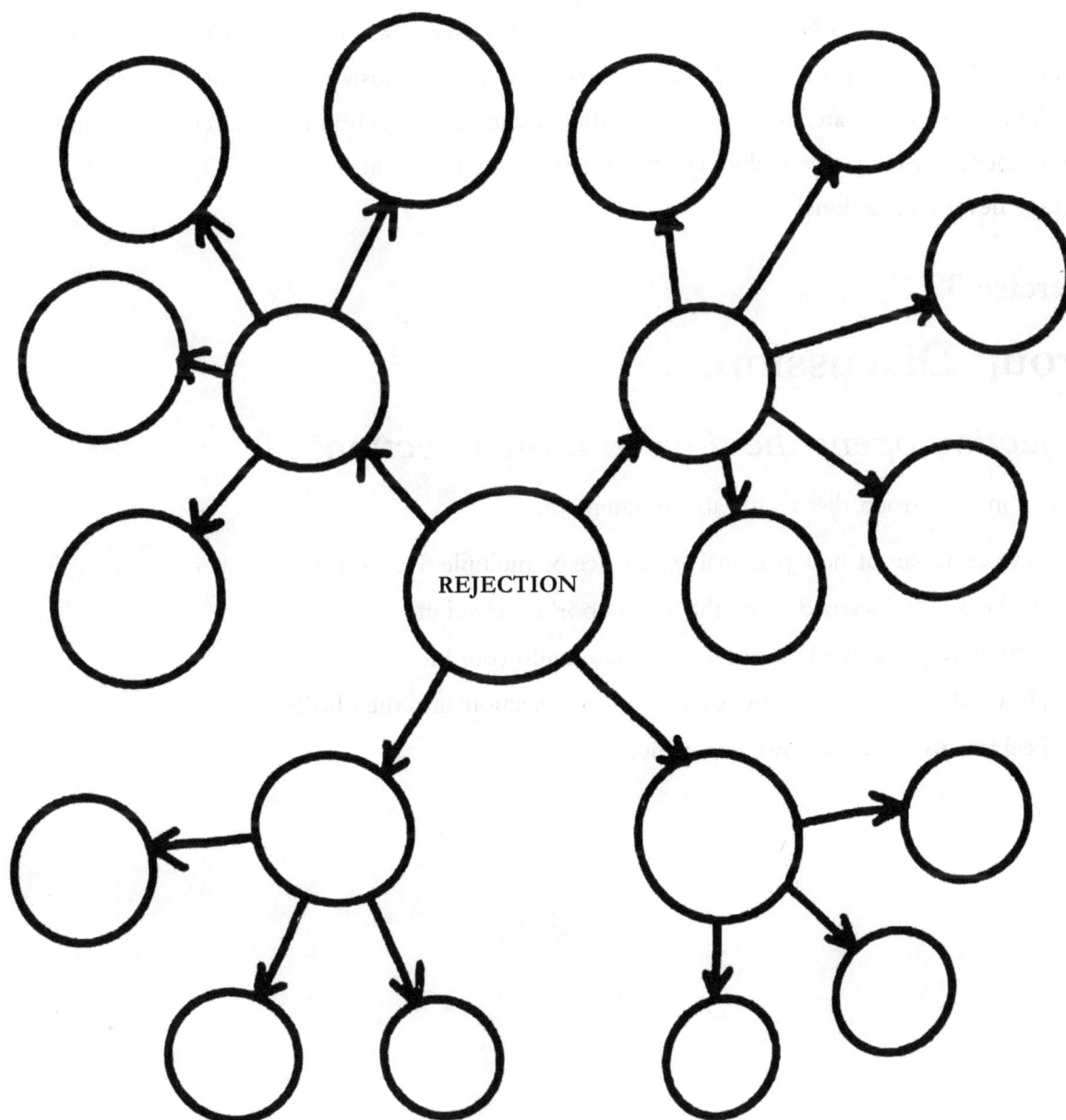

REJECTION

What is Rejection?

The world's definition of **'rejection'** is associated with words like 'denial', 'negative', 'denunciation', 'rebuff', etc.

The Bible's root word of the word 'rejected' (châdal) is to: **cease; forbear; leave; left off; let-alone; forbare; rest; unoccupied; wanteth;** and occurs at least 59 times in the Bible.

What does constant rejection do to a person?

Rejection can cause someone to pull away from others and can lead to feelings of loneliness, isolation, and depression. Constant rejection can adversely affect a person's mental health and well-being. An individual may be led to believe that 'rejection' is all they deserve, whether it be rejection from parents, friends, employment opportunities, hopes, dreams, and more seriously a feeling that Christ has rejected them. The symptoms related to rejection can often invite more rejection from other sources and lead to other mental health issues, including anxiety, stress, and personality disorders. The 'spirit of rejection' never travels alone!

Exercise 3

Group Discussion…

'Rejection opens the door to more rejection'

Alone or in your group, discuss the above statement.

- Give examples of how personal experience of multiple rejections can crush a woman's spirit.
- What have you learned about the 'open door' to rejection?
- How have you invited the spirit of rejection into your life?
- How did Adam and Eve invite the 'spirit of rejection' into their lives?
- Feel free to share your own experience.

Exercise 4

Without looking at page 60, explore the 'Root & Fruits of Rejection' tree below. Can you identify the 'fruits' of rejection growing in your life?

- Using the template on page 60, jot down what you believe are the root causes and the fruits of rejection in your life.

"...but a wounded spirit who can bear?"
Proverbs 18:14 (KJV)

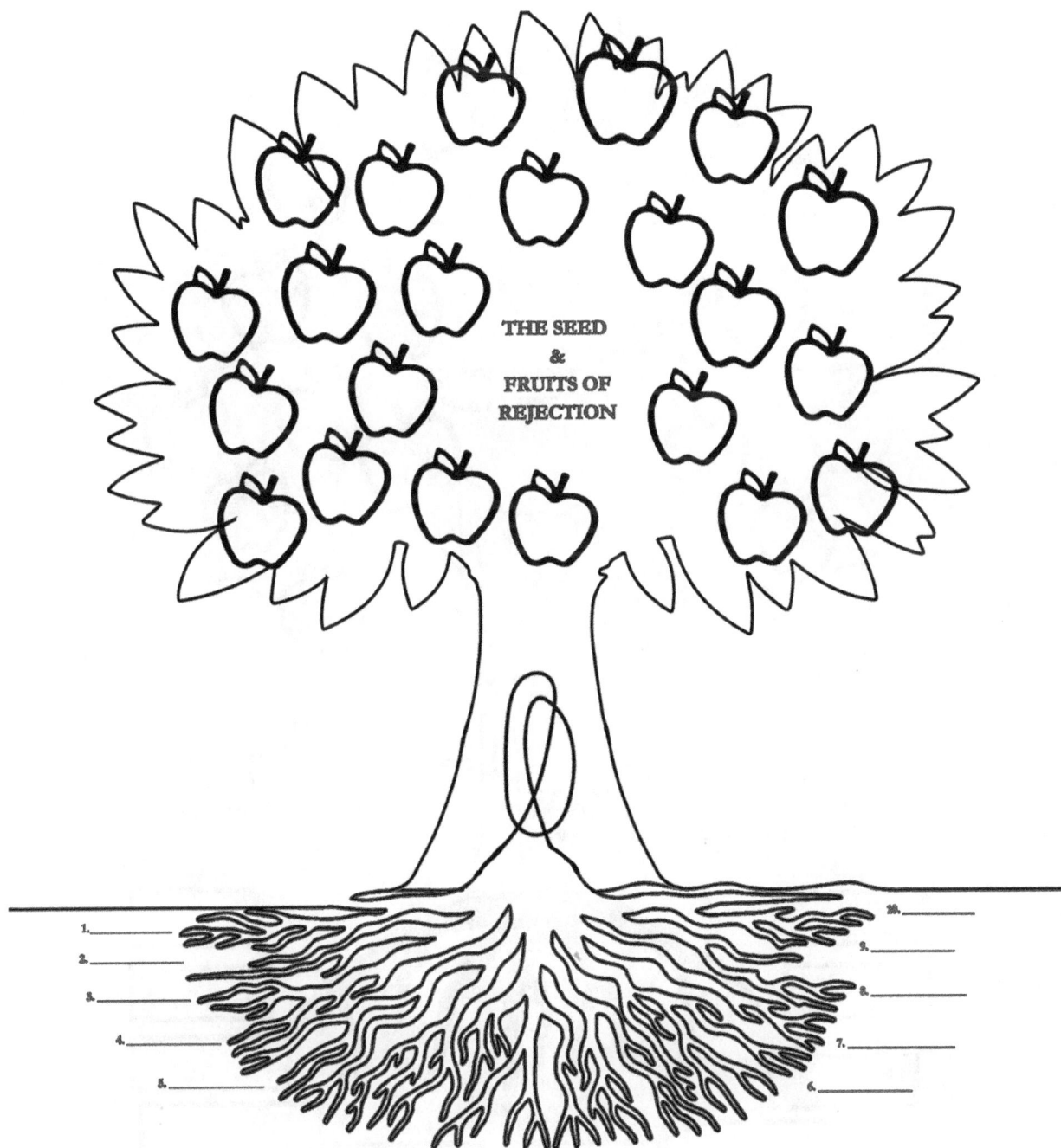

THE SEED
&
FRUITS OF
REJECTION

1._____
2._____
3._____
4._____
5._____

10._____
9._____
8._____
7._____
6._____

Exercise 5

The 'Fruits' of a Spirit of Rejection

"Every tree that bringeth not forth good fruit is hewn down and cast into the fire."

Matthew 7:19 (KJV)

Separation from Yeshua

Insecurity

Poor Self Image

Fear of Failure

Blame others

Reject others

Negative self talk

Lonliness

Aggression

Stubbornness

Competitive

THE FRUITS OF REJECTION

Low self esteem

Feeling Inferior

Withdrawal

Depression

Lack of Discernment

Self Condemnation

Self Centred

Feelings of Loss

Self Reliance

The roots of rejection - these can be minimal or severe dependent on the type(s)/duration of the rejection experienced by an individual.

Note down what you feel are the roots of rejection. The first one is done for you.

This is not an exhaustive list, please use the template to add more 'Reactions Symptoms & Measures'.

1. Parent(s) childhood

10.

2.

9.

3.

8.

4.

7.

5.

6.

Exercise 6 (Template)

Roots & Fruits of Rejection

Reflections:

_____

_____

_____

_____

_____

_____

_____

_____

_____

_____

_____

_____

_____

_____

_____

_____

From Genesis to Revelation...

In Genesis 3:6, we witness the origin of 'rejection'. Rejection of Yahweh's basic commandments, the blessed home He gave us and rest we would have benefited from, if it were not for Adam and Eve's disobedience (Genesis 2:17).

In the New Testament, we see first-hand how Adam and Eve's fall from grace gave permission to Satan to introduce far deadlier spirits on earth.

Let us consider Mary Magdalene, who was possessed by seven evil spirits in Luke 8: 1-2 (KJV):

> *"And it came to pass afterward,*
> *that he went throughout every city and village,*
> *preaching and shewing the glad tidings of the kingdom of God:*
> *and the twelve were with him,*
> [2] *And certain women, which had been healed of evil spirits and infirmities,*
> *Mary called Magdalene, out of whom went seven devils."*

Exercise 7

Group Discussion

- Consider how Mary Magdalene must have lived before being healed by Christ?
- How might her community have viewed/treated her?
- Do you see any similarities between your life experience and Mary Magdalene (only share what you are comfortable with sharing)?
- Consider your earliest experience of 'rejection'; how did this experience shape your life today?

Often, when we experience one form of rejection and do not fully recover spiritually, emotionally, and physically, it opens the door to other unclean spirits.

Read the case study found on page 63. Then, answer the questions. Be prepared to give feedback or share with a sister in Christ.

Exercise 8

Read the following case together or on your own.

The Case of 'Maria'

Let's consider Maria… (This is a true story, but names have been changed to protect their identity.)

Maria was often the 'outsider' in her home and at school. Her mother would remind her that she was 'unplanned' and a 'mistake'. These harsh words took a toll on Maria, and as a result she struggled academically and found it challenging to develop long and meaningful relationships with others throughout her life.

Maria was always in the lower learning sets at school, but she was extremely bright and loved to read. Maria was never assessed for dyslexia or for any other learning difficulty. The children at school often called her 'stupid', so Maria would often play alone or with one other girl whom her classmates also considered 'stupid'. Throughout school, Maria worked hard not to show her feelings or express her anger at being unfairly treated.

As an adult, Maria became the 'nice girl' at college and work. Nothing was ever too much trouble (or so she would say). Maria was overlooked several times for promotions (which she knew she deserved) because she worked hard and dedicated her life to work and others. To compensate for her disappointment, she consoled herself by saying, "It's not Yahweh's will for me at the moment."

From the moment she left college, she would often date undesirable men who would abuse her physically, verbally, and mentally. Maria became increasingly depressed and despondent about her life and began to self-harm. Maria also attempted suicide on two occasions. Maria struggled to reach out for help to her church brothers and sisters, as she felt nobody would want to help. Maria always felt her problems were insignificant to others.

In pairs…

- Jot down in your notebook the significant events that affected Maria's life.
- Identify where you believe the 'Spirit of Rejection' entered Maria's life.
- Identify any additional unclean spirits that entered after Maria's initial rejection experience.
- Identified Maria's ungodly responses and behaviours that followed, following the unjust treatment towards Maria throughout her life.

Reflection Point...

Neurologists have written about the effects of 'rejection' on our physical pain pathways in the brain. Numerous MRI studies show that the area of the brain that becomes activated when we experience rejection is the same area that is activated when we experience physical pain. **What does this show you about the effects of 'rejection' in our lives? Yes, rejection can be extremely painful.**

Signs and Symptoms of Rejection

Fear of rejection can lead to co-dependency, clingy, obsessive, jealous, or angry behaviour in relationships. **Self-rejection** can make you drive others away, leading to loneliness and depression (please revisit the 'Rejection Tree' on page 60 to remind you). Rejection can lead to you rejecting others to avoid being rejected yourself.

On your own...

Use the 'Rejection Tree' template on page 60 and prayerfully reflect on **one** significant experience of rejection. To get to the 'root of the problem', reflect on your earliest experience of feeling rejected. Often, the way we deal with rejection in our adult lives is most likely based on an early experience of rejection, i.e. being given up for adoption may lead to us feeling rejected and unwanted. As we grow up, we may seek experiences that validate this lie. Remember, Christ Yeshua described Satan as the 'father of lies' (John 8:44).

Yahweh declares, "We are fearfully and wonderfully made," (Psalm 139:14). If you are unsure of Yahweh's truth, revisit chapter 2.

Exercise 9

In pairs/threes or with a trusted sister in Christ

Share your findings from your rejection tree.

Focus on:

- Your experience of rejection.
- How you physically felt when you were rejected?
- What were you feeling at the time?
- What were you thinking?
- What do you believe about your experience of rejection?
- How have you coped with day-to-day life because of these experiences?
- How have your feelings of rejection hindered your spiritual progress?
- What rejecting words, statements, or declarations did you speak over yourself?

- What have you learned about your own signs, symptoms, and reaction to rejection?
- How is Christ speaking to you about these painful experiences?
- Do you find yourself responding in ungodly ways? If so, why?
- Write about it in your journals.
- How is Christ Yeshua speaking to you about these painful areas of rejection?

If you do not have time (if working in a group), continue to write about this in your reflective journal.

Reflections:

_____

_____

_____

_____

_____

_____

_____

_____

_____

_____

_____

_____

Biblical Roots when exploring 'Rejection'

The curse of rejection came with the fall of Adam and Eve. Adam and Eve lost the security of complete acceptance by Yahweh, as they rejected His instructions.

This first initial experience of rejection affects our lives profoundly. Rejection of Abba Father gave licence for our enemy Satan to curse mankind with a spirit of rejection. Adam and Eve were rejected from their safe home, Eden. Creation was sent into disarray; sin entered the world.

Therefore, the experience of rejection and acceptance comes primarily from our earliest human experiences and may be reinforced throughout our lives. This is why a feeling of being wanted and needed by our parents, mirrors how Abba Father feels about all His children.

When we experience abandonment, betrayal, and disappointment in relationships, we often relate this to feelings of rejection. If the rejection is severe, we can display and experience spiritual, emotional, physical, and mental symptoms. We may even experience physical pain.

The consequences of **rejection** for a Christian Woman can result in:

1. A strained relationship with Christ, the Godhead, and others. (Genesis 3:16-19).
2. Confusion with your identity in Christ. (Ephesians 2:3).
3. Emotional wounds can lead to ungodly behaviour. (Ephesians 4:26)
4. Self-rejection may manifest in harmful habits, such as engaging in pornography or overeating.
5. It can create a defensive attitude towards others, preventing you from receiving wise counsel. This can open the door to a spirit of pride. (Proverbs 11:2).
6. Withdrawal from fellowship with your brothers and sisters in Christ.
7. Intensified feelings of loneliness and isolation.
8. The emergence of a "victim spirit."
9. Inability to pursue your calling.
10. A risk of losing your faith in Christ.
11. Ultimately, the possibility of walking away from Christ.
12. Spiritual, mental, and physical wounds can breed anger towards Yahweh, distancing you from Christ Yeshua and causing you to shy away from being near Him due to your fear of rejection.

You must recognise and confront these consequences to reclaim your identity and relationship with Christ.

Fact...

At His crucifixion, Christ cried out in a loud voice saying, 'Eli, Eli, lama sabachthani?' This is translated as, 'My God, my God, why hast thou forsaken me?' (Matthew 27:45-53 KJV) Abba Father rejected His Son so we may be reconciled to Him. When the Prince of Peace rose again on the third day, we were no longer rejected. Christ made a way for us to be accepted if we desired a relationship with the Godhead.

Why do we need to freely accept Christ?

Let me direct you to another piece of scripture where Peter denied Christ three times (Luke 22:54-62)? For Peter to be reconciled to Christ and be forgiven, Christ had to ask Peter three times if he loved Him (John 21:15-17). In asking Peter three times, Christ was reversing the curse of Peter's rejection of Him three times before he was crucified on the cross. Not only did Christ forgive Peter, but Christ also blessed him with his ministry.

When we say 'yes' to Christ we are reversing the curse of Adam and Eve originating in the Garden of Eden. We are being obedient to His word.

You see, there is hope and freedom from rejection for daughters in Christ!

GENERATIONAL REJECTION

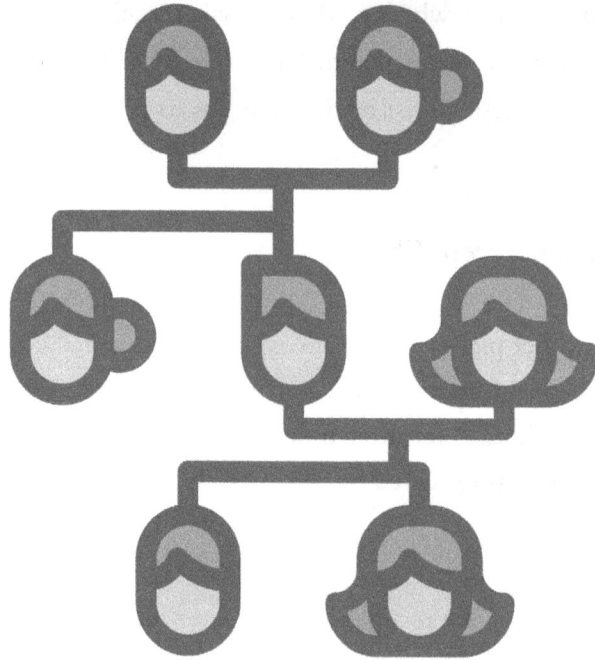

Signs You Are Battling ➔ with A Spirit of Rejection

1. You find yourself comparing your circumstances or situations with others, and you never seem to measure up.

2. You continually feel like you have missed out on life's opportunities and now it's too late.

3. No amount of encouragement is enough to convince you of your worth.

4. You feel rejected if you are not acknowledged by others.

5. You constantly seek the approval of others and seek to please others at the expense of your own needs and that of your familiy's.

6. You are easily offended, defended or embarrassed by discipline or correction.

7. You are always trying to prove yourself in public.

8. You feel like an outsider when interacting with others.

9. You think you could do a better job than others, if given the opportunity to do so.

10. You believe no-one understands you or what you are going through.

11. Endless 'doom scrolling' on social media, as you compare yourself and your life to others.

12. You adjust your personality to fit in.

How Do We Cope?

In response to experiencing rejection, we may begin to develop and exhibit behaviours that help us to cope. Rejection can feel very painful, and because of this we deal with our pain in ungodly ways.

1. **We may:**
   - Repress or dismiss our feelings.

   - **Respond in unhealthy ways, such as:**
     - Crying excessively (note that crying can also be used manipulatively to prevent others from correcting us).
     - Becoming angry over minor issues.
     - Hurting ourselves or others.
     - Using silence as a form of manipulation to keep others at a distance.
     - Refusing constructive feedback.

2. **We might try to fill the pain of rejection with:**
   - Food.
   - Sex.
   - Material possessions.
   - Excessive exercise or activities.
   - Overworking.
   - Engaging in 'dangerous or unhealthy behaviours'.

At the root of our feelings of rejection often lies anger. Rejected and hurt individuals frequently experience anger to some degree. Unresolved anger can hinder our healing process. Sometimes, we might even reject others before they can reject us, believing it gives us a sense of control; however, this behaviour only underscores the depth of our pain regarding potential rejection.

For instance, a partner who feels rejected may create a circumstance that allows them to end a relationship before their partner does. They think this will improve their self-image by enabling them to feel in control, but it mainly highlights their fear of rejection.

If you are struggling with rejection, you may also be grappling with unforgiveness toward yourself and others (see Galatians 6:7-9, Hebrews 12:14-15, and Matthew 7:12). If these feelings remain unaddressed, we risk:
   - Self-harm.
   - Becoming a people-pleaser.

- Developing unhealthy habits.
- Denying our genuine emotions.
- Creating perfectionist tendencies to seek acceptance.
- Engaging in cycles of rejection that may lead to rebellion to hide our pain.
- Rebelling against our relationship with God (Abba Father).
- Allowing rebellion to foster prideful thinking, (Proverbs 14:12).
- Making ourselves the centre of attention and inviting a 'victim mentality' into our lives.
- Finding it almost impossible to build meaningful relationships, leading us to choose solitude.

Can you recognise any of your behaviours in the statements above?

Exercise 10

In pairs, discuss...

1. Which behaviours resonate with you and why?

Write your reflections here:

....

....

....

....

....

....

....

....

....

....

The Antidote to Rejection is...
Acceptance

Christ Yeshua is our antidote for the 'spirit of rejection'. Christ's character is to be accepting. Christ died on the cross so the veil could be torn, so that through Him we could be reconciled to Yahweh. We do not need to work for our Salvation!

Yahweh is accepting of us all through His Son, Christ Yeshua. In the Old Testament Our Lord would remind his people (Israel) to walk and be obedient to His statutes. They struggled greatly. We too fail miserably, if it were not for the atonement of Christ. Christ took on our rejection. He was rejected by His Father, so we could be accepted by Our Father in heaven (John 19:28-30). Being accepting in the Kingdom of God results in eternal blessings.

So, we must:

1. Confess with our mouth that Christ Yeshua is your saviour and King.
2. Believe in your heart that Yahweh raised Christ from the dead, you will be saved (Romans 10:9 (NKJV).
3. Share your testimony with others (Revelation 12:11).
4. Abide and live by His word.

The reward for believing His instructions in faith is that you will never be put to shame (Romans 10:11). Our Father in heaven asks us to accept Christ Yeshua unconditionally, so that we can be accepted by Him. What a divine exchange!

Remember Ephesians 1:4 (KJV) tells us that:

> *"According as he hath chosen us in him before the foundation of the world, that we should be holy and without blame before him in love."*

Rejection hurts but the pain and reality of how we feel, must be faced. There is no getting away from it. If we do not face it, we will suppress it and develop ungodly ways to manage our responses to rejection.

Our ungodly behaviour(s) will become sinful – **Can you think why this might be?**
In not addressing our feelings of rejection in a godly way, we are rejecting the Word of Yahweh, and this is also a sin.

Christ Yeshua brings compassion, forgiveness, healing, and comfort into our rejections. Allowing ourselves to experience His compassion enables us to forgive those who have hurt us, and to forgive ourselves, too.

It is time to close the door and evict the 'Spirit of Rejection' in our lives.

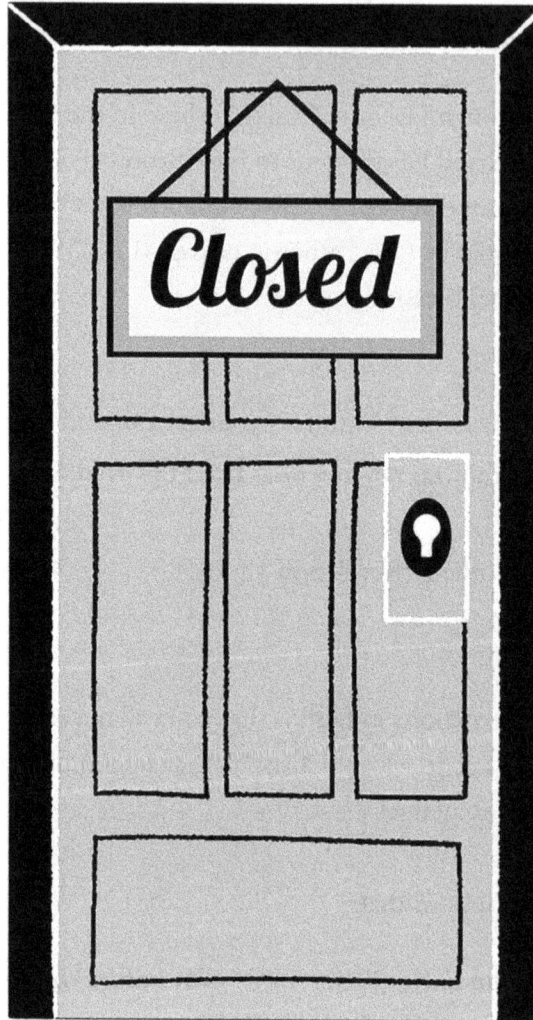

Matthew 19:26 (KJV)

"But Jesus beheld them, and said unto them,
With men this is impossible; but with God all things are possible."

Why do we need to remember this?

How do we begin to heal from rejection?

Scripture tells us that Satan is a created being (John 1:3). Yahweh created him. Therefore, Satan can torment us with the pain and trauma we have already experienced, as well as the generational sin on our family line. When we struggle to overcome these painful experiences, Satan and his army of fallen angels will use these painful experiences to kill, steal, and destroy us (John 10:10). We must take heed of the second part of this verse. **"Christ came so that we might have life and that we might have it more abundantly," (John 10:10).**

So, how do we resist the devil and close the door to his schemes?

1. We must confess and repent for our ungodly behaviours that resulted because of being rejected, (See James 5:16)
2. Forgiving those who we feel are responsible for our feelings of rejection.
3. Forgiving ourselves for wrongfully blaming or harming ourselves because of the rejection we feel.
4. Continual commitment to daily repentance and forgiveness of others and self.
5. Committing to putting on the armour of Yahweh to fight the enemies' schemes.
6. Asking Christ Yeshua to remind us of His acceptance of you, daily.
7. Seeking pastoral support from a prayer partner, prayer group, or Christian counsellor for the deeper wounds of rejection.

We will look at repentance and forgiveness in more detail in Module 7.

Call To Action

Dear Sister,

If you have managed to complete this chapter, well done. I can assure you that Christ is beginning His work in you and will see it through to its completion (Philippians 1:6). Amen!

You may not yet be a believer in Christ and have come across this book by divine appointment. You may be new to Christianity, and Christ is calling you to be a member of His worldwide family. You may be completing this workbook alone, or you may have been invited to join a Christian women's group to complete this workbook together. Whatever the reason, Christ wants to save you and redeem you from hell and eternity without Him.

Maybe you are already a professed Christian, but your Christian Walk has gone cold or is lukewarm. Remember what scripture says about the lukewarm Christian? *'I will spue thee out of my mouth.'* (Revelation 3:16 KJV)

If this describes you, it is not too late to invite/reinvite Christ Yeshua into your heart. To make Him your Lord and Saviour.

How might you do this?

Take your time and in a quiet space:

- Repent (express sincere regret or remorse about the sinful way you have lived).
- Ask Christ to forgive you and save you from the rightful penalty of eternal death (which you rightfully deserve).
- Confess with your mouth that Christ is Lord, 'and believe with your heart that Yahweh raised Christ Yeshua from the dead'. (Romans 10:9)
- If you willingly surrender and say this prayer, asking Christ Yeshua into your heart, spirit, soul, and mind, scripture says, 'You will be saved!'

There is some amazing news I want to share with you once you have decided to be a follower of Christ Yeshua. Luke 15:10 (KJV) says, **"Likewise, I say unto you, there is joy in the presence of the angels of God over one sinner that repenteth."**

Sister in Christ, Heaven is rejoicing!

Homework 3

Your homework has three parts to it this week, so please set enough time to prayerfully complete these tasks.

Materials you will need:

- **Bible**
- **Paper**
- **Pens**
- **Coloured pens or pencils**
- **Any other creative materials you would like for this task**

Part 1

- Set aside time to be with Christ Yeshua.
- Pray and seek guidance and protection from the Holy Spirit, if you feel emotional.
- Ask the Holy Spirit to identify the roots of your rejection. For a reminder, refer to the 'roots and fruits tree' exercise on page 60.
- Ask the Holy Spirit to minister to you and reveal His truth about each situation.
- Ask Christ Yeshua to bring His healing.

Part 2

- Complete a 'rejection' genogram – identify areas where this oppressive spirit came in.
- Prayerfully reflect on your genogram, asking the Holy Spirit to reveal any insights.
- Repent of any personal sinful thoughts, behaviours, and actions you have engaged in response to feeling rejected.
- Repent of any sinful actions your generational line has engaged in due to feeling rejected by self and others.
- Repent and forgive those involved and ask Abba Father to come in and heal the wounds.

Part 3

Creative work:

- Using creative materials, such as coloured pens, pencils, playdough, plasticine, etc., ask the Holy Spirit to give you an image of what the 'spirit of rejection' has done and how it is still impacting your life.
- Ask the Holy Spirit to give you an image of how Abba Father wants to heal you and close the door on your personal feelings of 'rejection'. **What would the 'accepted' image look like?**
- In doing this exercise, the Holy Spirit may reveal more thoughts and behaviours that you must repent of.
- Prayerfully ask for Christ to heal your broken heart, bind up your wounds, and wipe your tears away, (Isaiah 61:1).
- Prayerfully ask Abba Father to grow the fruits of the spirit in your life and to fill you anew with His Holy Spirit.

Homework Reflections

A Gift from Abba Father

"For ye have not received the spirit of bondage again to fear: but ye have received the Spirit of adoption, whereby we cry, Abba, Father."

Romans 8:15 (KJV)

END OF MODULE 3

MODULE 4
FREEDOM FROM FEAR

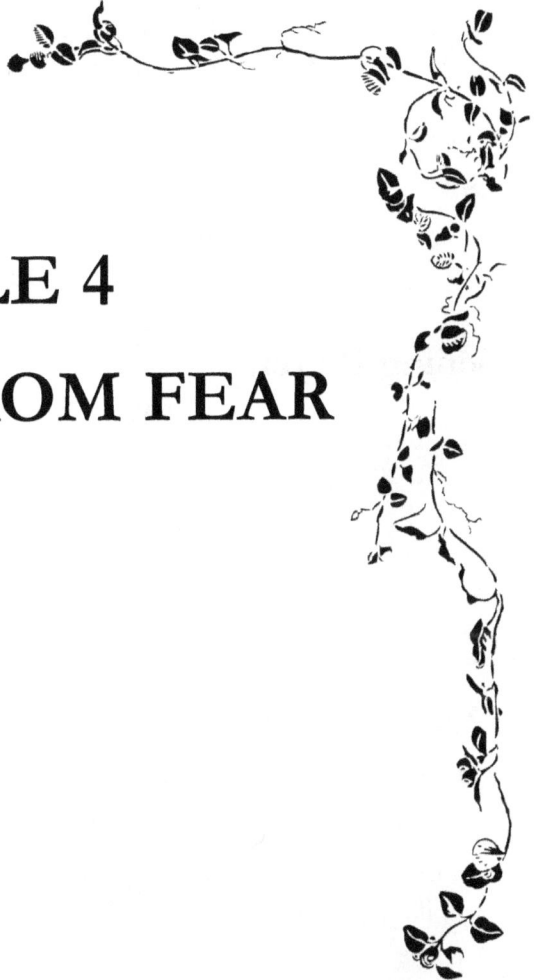

Module 4: Freedom From Fear

"For God hath not given us the spirit of fear;
but of power, and of love, and of a sound mind."
2 Timothy 1:7 (KJV)

Opening Prayer:

Group Contract:

If you are completing this programme within a group, I would strongly advise that you remind participants of the importance of adhering to and remaining committed to the group contract. Revisit the contract at the start of each session to ensure the safety of the group. It is important that the group adhere to it.

Session Aims

Explore personal meanings and experiences of fear as a daughter in Christ and God's plan of deliverance.

Session Outcomes

By the end of the session, delegates will be able to:
- Identify the roots of fear
- Examine personal meanings of fear
- Identify three or more ways fear has affected your life
- Differentiate between godly and ungodly fear
- Identify areas for the forgiveness of others and self

Module 4: This week we will be exploring the 'spirit of fear'.

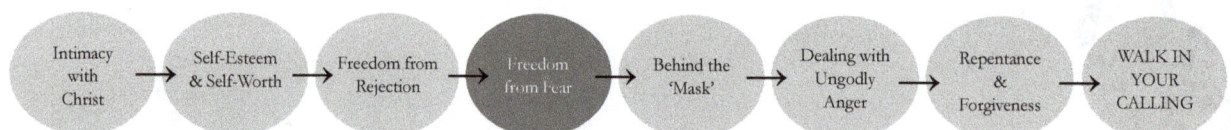

Intimacy with Christ → Self-Esteem & Self-Worth → Freedom from Rejection → Freedom from Fear → Behind the 'Mask' → Dealing with Ungodly Anger → Repentance & Forgiveness → WALK IN YOUR CALLING

Check-in (10 mins)

Delegates will share insights and reflections from session **3**.

- If working as a group, set aside 15-30 minutes to share your five-minute reflections on your creative homework in Module 3.
- Once you have all presented, spend five minutes discussing your learning.

Please keep to time boundaries.

Scripture Reading

Genesis 3: 8-10 (KJV)

"⁸ And they heard the voice of the Lord God walking in the garden in the cool of the day: and Adam and his wife hid themselves from the presence of the Lord God amongst the trees of the garden.

⁹ And the Lord God called unto Adam, and said unto him, Where art thou? ¹⁰ And he said, I heard thy voice in the garden, and I was afraid, because I was naked; and I hid myself."

Reflection Point

Exercise 1

On your own, in pairs/threes:

- How does this portion of scripture speak to you about nature and the root of fear?
- **Write your reflections below:**

....

....

....

....

....

....

....

....

....

....

Exploring the 'Spirit of Fear'

Introduction

In this module, we will look at overcoming fear in our lives, especially concerning the individual ministries Yahweh has chosen for us. For many women, walking in faith and fulfilling their ministry calling can be very difficult and challenging. Yahweh reveals His plan as we walk in faith, allowing us to see more and more of His plan unfolding that will bring glory to His name.

In Paul's Gospel, he is very clear that Yahweh gifts His children with the gifts of the Holy Spirit in preparation for work He has for us in His kingdom. However, there are countless daughters in Christ who do not allow Yahweh to do His work in them, because they have opened the door to the Spirit of Fear.

The Bible talks of a **"fearful spirit" (2 Tim, 1:7). This is very different from having a fear (reverence) for the Lord.** A 'spirit of fear' is an unclean spirit that comes against the Word of God; it seeks to challenge, question, and sow seeds of doubt in the believer's spirit, soul, and body. Opening the door to a 'spirit of fear' plants a seed of doubt; it allows generational curses to be fulfilled. Fear stops us from living a God-fulfilled life.

Exercise 2

Whether you are working alone or in a group; set aside five minutes to reflect on the following:

GROUP DISCUSSION

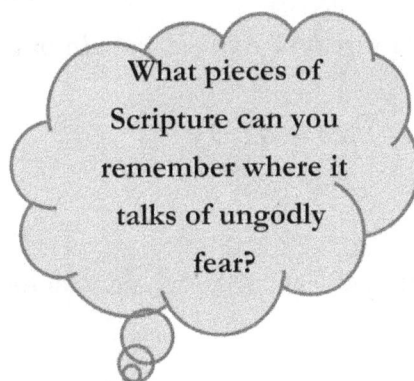

What pieces of Scripture can you remember where it talks of ungodly fear?

- **Write your reflections here:**

....

....

....

....

....

....

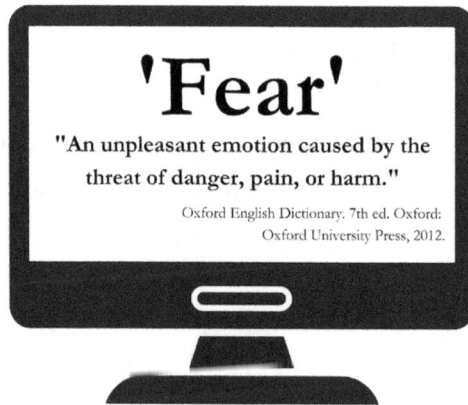

Definition

'Feelings of being under threat of danger, in pain or experiencing a sense of harm.'

Reflections (Group/Personal)

Exercise 3

- Name some of the thoughts and feelings associated with the word 'fear'.

....

....

....

....

Experiences Associated with Fear

- Worry: leading to feelings of resentment (Luke 10:41).
- Tension/pressure: feeling of stress.
- Fearfulness: sudden fear, common or violent terror; a feeling of apprehension.
- Fear of the future.
- Development of compulsive behaviours to combat feelings of fear.
- Anxiety: concerned about the future - (Matthew 6:25).
- Feelings of terror – (Luke 21:9).
- Displaced or dissociative thoughts and feelings

Exercise 4

- **Reflect on your own experiences of fear:**

....

....

....

....

....

....

....

....

....

....

....

Lecture...

All of us would have experienced 'fear' at some point in our lives. Fear can have a significant impact on how we live our lives. Fear can be debilitating.

A struggle to overcome a 'Spirit of Fear' means we are engaging with the enemy by allowing this spirit into our lives..

As with 'rejection', there are many worldly teachings on how to 'overcome fear', but for Christians the Bible is very clear about who and what operates behind a **'spirit of fear',** where it came from, and how it presents itself in the believer's life.

How 'fear' affects our Christian Walk:

1. Separates us from Yahweh which makes us vulnerable to Satan.
2. We believe that Yahweh cannot protect us.
3. We believe Satan is more powerful than Yahweh (Ezekiel 28:15).
4. We become separated from Yahweh's covering. Without His protection, the enemy can gain access to our lives (Ephesians 4:27-29).
5. It opens the door to other unclean spirits such as the 'spirit of rejection', a 'lying spirit', a 'spirit of infirmity', or a 'sprit of heaviness', etc.

Exercise 5: 'Roots and Fruits' of Fear

On your own and using the **'Roots and Fruits Tree of Fear'**, on page 88, reflect on:
1. How 'fear' shows up in your life and how the **'spirit of fear'** has prevented you from walking in your calling.

You can use the 'reflections' page to write down any thoughts the Holy Spirit brings to your mind. It may be helpful to reflect on your first experience of fear, because this is where the 'Spirit of Fear' has gained a foothold in your life (Ephesians 4:27-29). If we allow the enemy in, he will seek to set up residence in your heart, mind, soul and spirit.

Reflections:

The 'Roots & Fruits' of Fear

Exercise 6:

Identify the roots of these fruits of fear.

Blaming
Others

People
Pleasing

Poor Self
Image

Violence

Pretense

Reject
others

Negative
self talk

Contempt
for Self

Lonliness

Regret

Isolation

THE FRUITS
OF
FEAR

Feeling
Inferior

Abusing

Depression

Addictive
Behaviours

Low self
esteem

Eating
Disorders

Promiscuity

Anxiety

Self
Reliance

The roots of rejection
can be minimal or severe
dependent on the
type(s)/duration of the
rejection experienced by the
individual.

ROOT
CAUSES
that can
effect you
& your
family

This is not an exhaustive list,
please use the template to
add more
Reactions
Symptoms &
Measures

1. Separation from
Christ Yeshua

2. _____

3. _____

4. _____

5. _____

10. _____

9. _____

8. _____

7. _____

6. _____

WHAT ARE THE ROOT CAUSES OF FEAR
Identify why a Christian has a 'Spirit of Fear' - The first one is done for you.

The 'Roots & Fruits' of Fear

Exercise 7:

Using the template, complete the tree of 'roots and fruits' for your own life.

THE FRUITS
OF
FEAR

1._____
2._____
3._____
4._____
5._____

10._____
9._____
8._____
7._____
6._____

Reflections

Reflections

How a 'spirit of fear' affects my body?

FIGHT OR FLIGHT

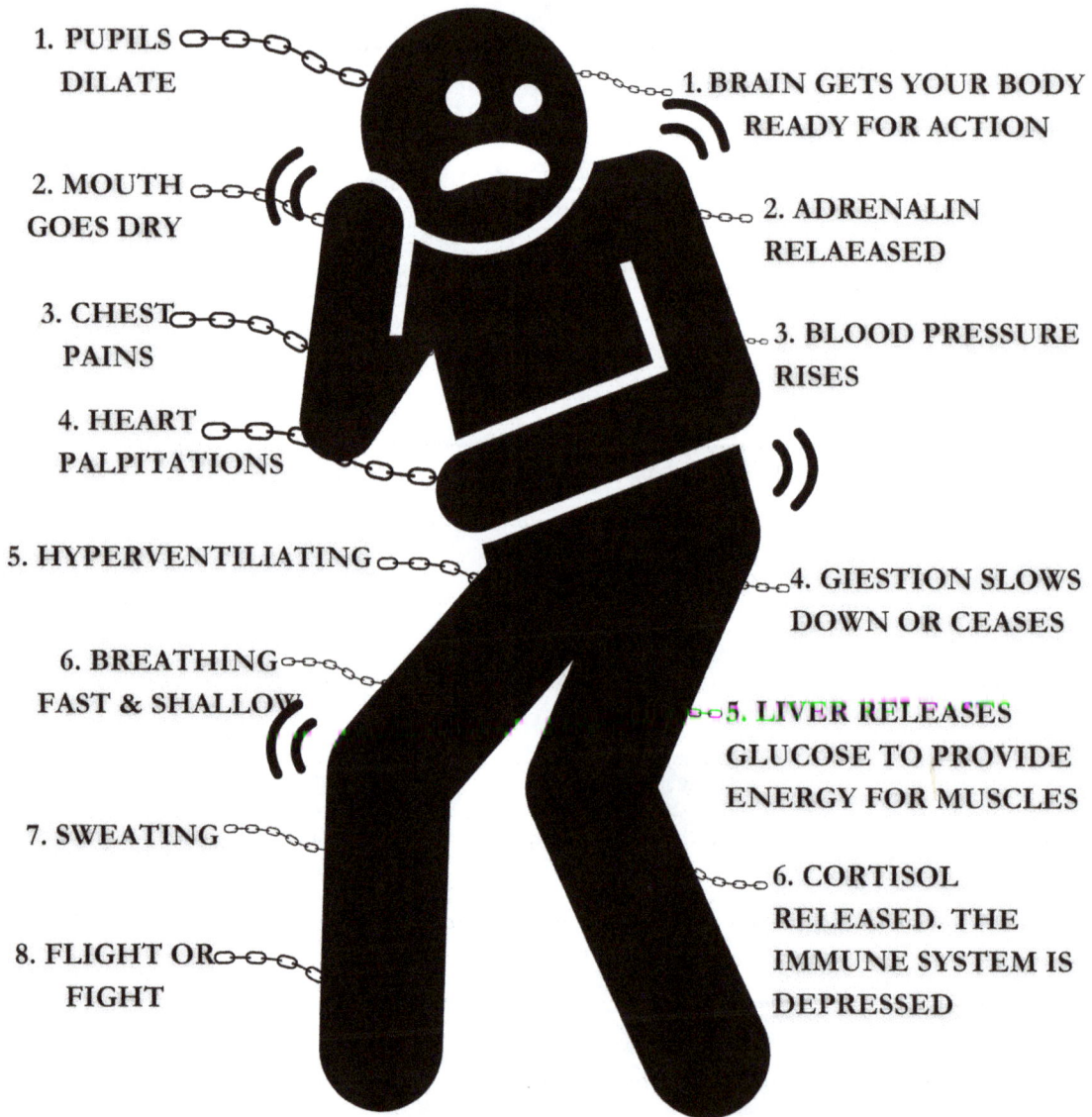

1. PUPILS DILATE

2. MOUTH GOES DRY

3. CHEST PAINS

4. HEART PALPITATIONS

5. HYPERVENTILIATING

6. BREATHING FAST & SHALLOW

7. SWEATING

8. FLIGHT OR FIGHT

1. BRAIN GETS YOUR BODY READY FOR ACTION

2. ADRENALIN RELAEASED

3. BLOOD PRESSURE RISES

4. GIESTION SLOWS DOWN OR CEASES

5. LIVER RELEASES GLUCOSE TO PROVIDE ENERGY FOR MUSCLES

6. CORTISOL RELEASED. THE IMMUNE SYSTEM IS DEPRESSED

Have you identified any other oppressive spirits that took their opportunity to attach themselves to your 'spirit of fear'?

How a 'spirit of fear' affects your Soul?

Fear locks us into specific, related, fearful behavioural responses, such as:

- Excessive worry (Ezekiel 2:6).
- Excessive need to behave compulsively without reason.
- Loss or lack of sleep (Psalm 127:2).
- Fearful thoughts seem to lead to other thoughts until they become out of hand.
- A lack of peace.
- A sense of paralysis that prevents you from engaging in day-to-day activities.

How a 'spirit of fear' affects your Spirit?

The Bible talks of the 'spirit of fear' affecting individuals by inviting related spirits such as a:

- A crushed spirit – Isaiah 61:1.
- An overwhelmed spirit – Psalm 142.
- A timid spirit – 2 Timothy 1:7.

The effect of a 'spirit of fear' on our behaviour towards others and self may lead to further ungodly behaviours that separate us from Abba Father.

Exercise 9

How has 'fear' affected your Soul & Spirit?

Write your reflections below.

....

....

....

....

....

Lecture: Godly Fear...

*"But now thus saith the Lord that created thee,
O Jacob, and he that formed thee, O Israel,
Fear not: for I have redeemed thee, I have called
thee by thy name; thou art mine."*
Isaiah 43:1 (KJV)

Recognising and differentiating between godly and ungodly fear is essential. From the beginning of time on earth, Yahweh has presented us, His children, with a way out. We see that at the fall the 'Spirit of rebellion (likened to witchcraft) 1 Samuel 15:23), rejection and fear' entered in as Adam and Eve ate the forbidden fruit. Immediately, they were aware they were naked, and their sin was revealed. They were **afraid** and hid from Yahweh. They had let Abba Father down and were fearful and ashamed. Yahweh's love is merciful, and through Christ (the way, truth and the life – John 14:6), the world was finally set free from the prince of this earth (Satan); we were set free from oppression, if we chose Christ to be our Saviour and honour his biblical rules and principles.

Godly fear warns us to avoid dangerous situations, i.e. the fight or flight response. However, we see the antidote to fear in John 12:27. The fear of the Lord is "Godly", the Bible says: *'7 The fear of the Lord is the beginning of knowledge,'* Proverbs 1:7 (KJV), and Proverbs 16:6 says, *"6 By mercy and truth iniquity is purged: and by the fear of the Lord men depart from evil."*

Having godly fear indicates reverence and obedience to the Godhead. Godly fear acknowledges Yahweh's omniscience and omnipresence, His awe, might, wonder, and splendour. Godly fear is a reverence of Yahweh's holiness. Being God-fearing helps us grow in wisdom, understanding, and faith.

When we fail to acknowledge the awesomeness of Yahweh, it is easy for us to fall into sin. Our reverence for the Godhead makes us want to worship and praise Him, as our spirit is no longer dead but alive to Christ (Romans 5:1-17).

Steps to Deliverance from a 'Spirit of Fear'

- Psalm 91 is the biblical antidote for overcoming fear and seeking to ensure we are under God's covering.
- Psalm 91 tells us that when we come underneath godly covering, we will not fear.
- When we are under Yehovah's covering, we are covered and protected from fear from our enemies.
- Phrases such as 'Do not fear', 'Do not be afraid', 'Fear not', etc., occur over three hundred times in the Bible. How awesome is that! So why do Christians continue to fear?
- The story of Gideon demonstrates how a man of God overcame a 'spirit of fear'.

What was the godly weapon used to overcome the 'spirit of fear' in Gideon?

Exercise 10

- Choose any of the scripture verses below and discuss how it speaks to your spirit about the nature of fear in your life.
- In addition to your homework, read the following scriptures: **Isaiah 8:12; 35:4; 41:10; Isaiah 41:13; 43:1; 51:7; Isaiah 54:4; Jeremiah 30:10; 46:27; 46:28, 1 Peter 3:6; 3:14.**

How to Renew Your Mind with The Word of God

Romans 12:2

Many of us have had to overcome ungodly habits in our lives, due to being fearful.

Ungodly behaviours and thinking can consist of:
- **Overeating/greed.**
- **Starving ourselves or adopting unhealthy eating habits.**
- **Self-harm.**
- **Erratic behaviour.**
- **Being irritable with self and others.**
- **Turning to alcohol or drugs.**
- **Communicating excessive anger in our words and actions.**
- **Engaging in excessive spending.**
- **Avoidance of prayer**
- **Refusing to rest and observe Yahweh's commandments on rest.**
- **Engaging in perverse sexual acts.**
- **Adopting a 'victim' mentality.**

However, when we accept Christ into our hearts, we choose to be an overcomer in Christ. We know there is a battle for our spirit, soul, and body, but we must say **'Yes'** to Christ's desire to heal and transform us.

Exercise 11

For example, if you have overcome a 'spirit of fear', reflect on the following:
- **How has Christ healed you, or is healing you?**
- **What was or has been the process?**
- **Which brother or sister in Christ did God bring alongside you to support you and offer wise counsel?**
- **What scripture verses did He give you?**
- **How did the Holy Spirit begin to renew your mind (Romans 12:2)?**
- **Are you now a new creation, or do you still battle with old habits and ungodly behaviours?**
- **How has Christ used you to help others with a 'spirit of fear'?**
- **Are you testifying to Yahweh's grace in your life? If not, why not?**

Reflections

Exercise 12

On your own or in pairs, share one struggle you are experiencing with 'fear' (there may be more fears to share, but you can share these outside of the classroom). You will have 10 minutes each to explore the questions below. James 5:16 (KJV) encourages to ***"Confess your faults one to another, and pray one for another, that ye may be healed. The effectual fervent prayer of a righteous man availeth much."***

Group Work

Let me remind you of the importance of confidentiality. Unless your sister in Christ discloses harm to self or others, participation in drug trafficking or participation in terrorism activities, you must **not** share their story without their permission. However, I would encourage you to share your own testimony with others as much as you can (Revelation 12:11).

Remember, Satan wants you to keep this secret so he can torment you and make accusations about you before Yahweh night and day (Revelation 12:10).

Exercise 13

This is a self-test

Read the statements below, look up the verse, and meditate on your personal application. On the line, make a (tick) √ if the statement characterises you currently. If it does not, continue to meditate on what changes you need to make, and pray for Christ's help in changing those things. Be open to receiving godly counsel concerning all areas that you need guidance for.

You may also want to mediate on one **'Fear Not'** verse per day, until it is written on your heart and in your mind. Ask yourself: Do I believe in what scripture says?

As a 'God-fearing' daughter in Christ, I am and can demonstrate evidence of: (please tick all that apply)

- ☐ 1. Yahweh's instruction in my life choices (Psalm 25:12).
- ☐ 2. Being blessed with prosperity in many ways (Psalm 25:13).
- ☐ 3. Experiencing Yahweh's compassion (Psalm 103:11-18).
- ☐ 4. Yahweh's loving grace and His generosity towards me and others (Psalm 112:4-5).
- ☐ 5. Being confident and courageous (Psalm 112:6-8; Pr 14:26).
- ☐ 6. Being content and feeling at peace (Proverbs 19:23).
- ☐ 7. Being confident that my prayers will be heard and answered (Psalm 145:19).
- ☐ 8. Being blessed with wisdom (Proverbs 1:7; 9:10).
- ☐ 9. Being teachable and peaceful (Proverbs 8:13)
- ☐ 10. Demonstrating integrity and faithfulness (Job 2:3).
- ☐ 11. Being considerate and kind towards others (Psalm 112:4-5).

☐ 12. Being patient, hopeful, and genuine (Psalm 147:11).

☐ 13. Being responsible for my family (Psalm 128:3).

☐ 14. Being able to worship Yahweh openly (Revelation 14:7).

☐ 15. Not being afraid of man (Proverbs 29:25).

☐ 16. Being willing to leave, my job, family to go where the Lord leads me (Genesis 12:1).

Can you think of any more examples? Once you have completed the questionnaire and totalled your score out of 16, work in pairs or with a prayer partner to discuss your responses and areas for development. Write your reflections in the section below.

The Antidote...

How can we begin to renew our minds with the guidance and help from the Holy Spirit? Here are some godly tips to help you.

- Read and meditate on 2 Colossians 5:17 and Galatians 5:22-23.
- Seek knowledge from Christ Yeshua about your struggle with fear (where did it enter?).
- Please be sure to be real about the extent of your worries. Let Christ in! Remember our 'House Exercise' on page 14. Are you honest with the Lord about your fears?
- Truly repent for engaging with a 'spirit of fear'. Remember Yahweh told us to 'fear not' at least 33 times in His Word.
- Forgive yourself and others for opening the door to the 'spirit of fear'.
- Commit to facing the problem head-on, with Christ on your side.
- Seek Yahweh's guidance for a prayer/accountability partner (if you need one).
- Ask God to develop your discernment of Satan's lies concerning your fearful behaviours.
- Prayerfully, re-evaluate your identity in Christ.
- Read Romans 12:22. **How do you intend to renew your mind and change your thinking?**
- Continually ask the Holy Spirit to reveal any lies you still believe.
- Our ability to receive peace depends upon faith, trust, belief, and knowing Christ Yeshua calmed the storm. Peace equals faith and trust in Yahweh (Mark 4:35 to 41).
- **Can you think of any more godly habits you can develop to renew your mind and overcome a spirit of fear?**

Reflections

Call To Action

Dear Sister,

If you have managed to complete this chapter, well done. I can assure you that Christ is beginning His work in you and will see it through to its completion (Philippians 1:6). Amen!

You may not yet be a believer in Christ and have come across this book by divine appointment. You may be new to Christianity, and Christ is calling you to be a member of His worldwide family. You may be completing this workbook alone, or you may have been invited to join a Christian women's group to complete this workbook together. Whatever the reason, Christ wants to save you and redeem you from hell and eternity without Him.

Maybe you are already a professed Christian, but your Christian Walk has gone cold or is lukewarm. Remember what scripture says about the lukewarm Christian? *'I will spue thee out of my mouth.'* (Revelation 3:16 KJV)

If this describes you, it is not too late to invite/reinvite Christ Yeshua into your heart. To make Him your Lord and Saviour.

How might you do this?
Take your time, and in a quiet space:
- Repent (express sincere regret or remorse about the sinful way you have lived).
- Ask Christ to forgive you and save you from the rightful penalty of eternal death (which you rightfully deserve).
- Confess with your mouth that Christ is Lord, 'and believe with your heart that Yahweh raised Christ Yeshua from the dead' (Romans 10:9).
- If you willingly surrender and say this prayer, asking Christ Yeshua into your heart, spirit, soul, and mind, scripture says, 'You will be saved!'

There is some amazing news I want to share with you once you have decided to be a follower of Christ Yeshua. Luke 15:10 (KJV) says, **"Likewise, I say unto you, there is joy in the presence of the angels of God over one sinner that repenteth."**

Sister in Christ, Heaven is rejoicing!

Homework 4

Spend time with Christ Yeshua in prayer and conversation.

Write a letter to Christ Yeshua addressing the following points. **Get real with Yahweh!**

- The fears in my life that I allow to have control over me.

- What events in my life gave the 'spirit of fear' this opportunity?

- Ask Yahweh to link the relevant memory to the feelings of fear. Has 'fear' been a constant theme throughout your life?

- Ask Yeshua to expose the lies behind lies believed and reveal his truth. Agree with Yahweh that you will not be enslaved to fear.

- Write out some scriptures and have them handy if you begin to feel oppressed (Put on the armour of Yahweh).

- Begin to walk in freedom.

Reflections

END OF WORKBOOK 4

MODULE 5
BEHIND THE MASK

Module 5: Behind The Mask

*"She openeth her mouth with wisdom; and in
her tongue is the law of kindness."*
Proverbs 31.26 (KJV)

Opening Prayer:

Group Contract:

If you are completing this programme within a group, I suggest that you remind participants of the importance of adhering to and remaining committed to the group contract. Revisit the contract at the start of each session to ensure the group's safety. The group must adhere to it.

Session Aims

Explore the **'Masks'** we wear before Yahweh and with other people.

Session Outcomes

By the end of the session, you will be able to:

- Identify hidden aspects of your identity that you present to others, and the aspects of self that you want to conceal.
- Identify aspects of yourself using the mask template.
- Explore how wearing a mask separates us from feeling Yahweh's love.
- How wearing a mask opens us up to deceitful spirits and sinful behaviour.

Session 5: This week, we will explore 'The Masks We Wear'.

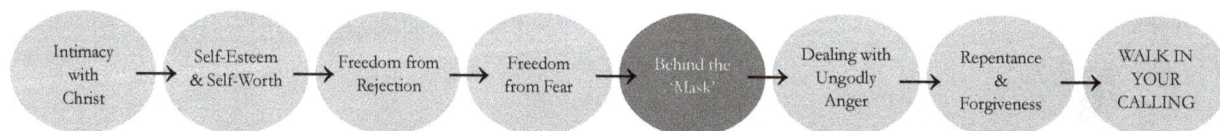

Intimacy with Christ → Self-Esteem & Self-Worth → Freedom from Rejection → Freedom from Fear → Behind the 'Mask' → Dealing with Ungodly Anger → Repentance & Forgiveness → WALK IN YOUR CALLING

Check-in (10mins)

Delegates will share insights and reflections from session 4.

- If working as a group, set aside 15–30 minutes to share your reflections gained from Module 4. **Please keep to time boundaries.**

Scripture Reading

Proverbs 26:24-28

"*24 He that hateth dissembleth with his lips, and layeth
up deceit within him;*
*25 When he speaketh fair, believe him not: for there are seven
abominations in his heart.*
*26 Whose hatred is covered by deceit, his wickedness shall
be shewed before the whole congregation.*
*27 Whoso diggeth a pit shall fall therein: and he that rolleth a stone,
it will return upon him. 28 A lying tongue hateth those that are
afflicted by it; and a flattering mouth worketh ruin.*"

Personal Reflection Point

Exercise 1

On your own, in pairs/threes:

- How does this piece of scripture speak to you about the nature of Christians who choose to wear masks?
- **Write your reflections below:**

....

....

....

....

....

....

....

....

....

Exploring 'Masks'

In this exercise, we will be looking at the masks we wear to separate ourselves from Yahweh and others.

What is a 'Mask'?

A mask is usually described as covering that shields the face and can be used to disguise your identity.

The Hebrew meaning of mask **(māšāl)** is interpreted as **'disguise' or 'idol'.** Yes, a mask can become an idol.

Exercise 2

Group Discussion/Personal reflection...
Why do people wear masks?

- _____

- _____

- _____

- _____

- _____

- _____

- _____

- _____

Why people wear masks?

Many times, throughout our lives, we wear masks that we want others to see. Sometimes we wear these masks with ourselves! We do not want others to see the wrong side of us, or see our weaknesses, we only want others to see the 'good side' of our personality and the personality that others around us want us to be. In effect we are lying to ourselves and others.

We convince ourselves that if we are what everyone else wants us to be, we will be accepted and liked. The problem with this is, there will come a time when our 'mask' will slip, revealing our true selves. You believe that being authentic will result in you being rejected.

Why, then, would this be a problem?

- You will suffer from exhaustion as you struggle to be yourself and someone else at the same time.
- There will always be someone who will know the 'true you'.
- There will come a time when you cannot hide behind the 'mask' any longer.
- Your 'authentic' self may not be liked by those around you, leading to rejection.
- You develop a 'split personality' otherwise known as a dissociative disorder.
- You have worn a 'mask' for such a long time, you don't know who you really are.
- You may enjoy wearing the 'mask' and lying to others.

Can you think of any other reasons?

- _____
- _____
- _____
- _____

Exercise 3

Types of Masks

1. Write down which of these descriptions describes you? (There may be more than one): _____.

2. Can you think of any more labels for this mask?

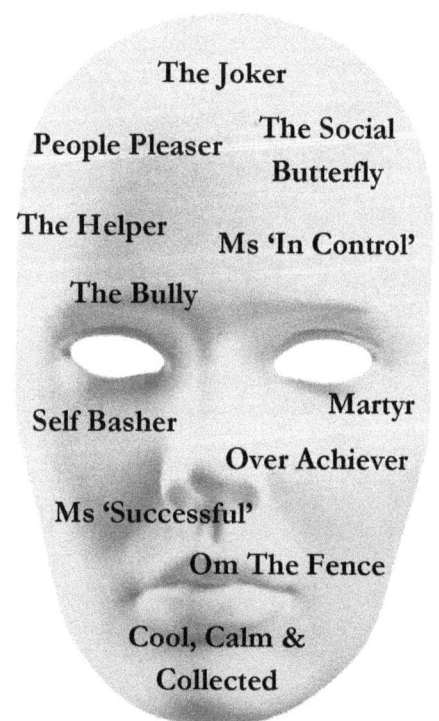

The Joker

People Pleaser

The Social Butterfly

The Helper

Ms 'In Control'

The Bully

Self Basher

Martyr

Over Achiever

Ms 'Successful'

Om The Fence

Cool, Calm & Collected

Let us look at some examples of masks we hide behind.

1. Sister 'Cool, Calm & Collected'

This sister in Christ remains cool, calm and collected in all situations. Nothing bothers her, neither conflict nor chaos; she always claims how 'calm and easy going' she is. However, you may witness 'spirit of anger' rear its ugly head when she cannot suppress these feelings anymore. Suppression of her true feelings often results in an emotional breakdown or severe illness. Her anger and frustration spew out like a volcano when she loses control, often adversely affecting those around her. Everybody gets it!

Is this you? _____

2. Sister 'Joker'

Humour can be used as a defence to hide how we truly feel about a situation. This is more commonly known as a 'defence mechanism'. Such defences defend us from the true pain we feel. Humour can also prevent intimacy because everything is a joke.

Sister Joker you will tell a joke to:

- Skirt around sincere discussions and try to keep it light-hearted.
- Keep conversations from getting too real or deep.
- Avoid confrontation, as humour serves as a protective shield.

A 'joker' will not allow anyone in, and this often results in loneliness.

Is this you? _____

3. Sister 'Perfectionist'

Sister Perfectionist unconsciously pursues perfectionism as a defence against feelings of failure. If everything is done right, then her world cannot fall apart. Perfectionism can elicit praise and recognition, but this only provides temporary relief. Sister Perfectionist lives under constant stress because everything must be perfect. Her perfectionism often separates her from those who are close to her and fosters an environment of stress and anxiety.

Is this you? _____

4. Sister 'Saint'

Sister Saint boasts that she single-handedly runs the church with her selfless actions. She is highly compassionate towards others and is always ready and willing to offer families and friends a compassionate ear, day or night. Her 'compassionate ear' is often a protective cover from working on herself or not admitting that she feels unworthy to receive help herself.

'Saints' often rely on other people's acknowledgement of their excellent work, and they often get angry if their work is not acknowledged. The Saint assumes that their part is vital and that the church will not exist without them! At times, there is an air of superiority about them that can make others uncomfortable because they cannot match their martyrdom.

'Saints' struggle to be in a relationship with others, as they are busy doing 'saintly' work. Martyrs often find themselves exhausted from martyr work as they volunteer for any role that needs doing in the fellowship, family, in fact anywhere they can put their 'saintly' paws on. The 'martyr' cannot be honest about their need for praise.

Is this you? _____

5. Sister 'Bully'

Every environment where we work, and play reflects the primary/secondary school playground. The playground was not always a source of fun and joy; for some, it was a place of hurt and harassment. Bullies can operate overtly or covertly, employing their bullying tactics. Bullies seek to gain control over others and situations using manipulation, domination, or aggression. Sometimes, their tactics can be physical and even fatal.

Whilst **'Sister Bully'** appears to be confident, beneath this confident mask she is infact insecure and suffers with low self-esteem and self-worth. Sister Bully seeks to gain respect from others through her bullying behaviour but does not realise that she does not respect herself. Sister Bully has little regard for anyone else and leaves behind her a trail of destruction and hurt.

Is this you? _____

6. Sister 'Controller'

'Sister Controller' uses order and power to achieve a sense of security. A close relative of Sister Bully, Sister Controller seeks to ensure that everything is in its proper place. This relieves her fear of the unknown, of ambiguity, of uncertainty. Sister Controller sees herself as the mother hen of all hens and will not let anyone out of her sight. Churchgoers may mistake her for the Pastor, as she has so much control over everyone and everything. Sister Controller becomes unnerved when others decide to break free from her and can feel highly wounded.

Is this you? _____

7. Sister 'Put-Down'

Suffering from unworthiness and insecurity, **'Sister Put-Down'** will project a negative view of herself onto others. She believes that she can protect herself from hurt by hurting herself first, often thinking, "I'll get myself first, before they get me!" This is all to protect herself against any potential criticism targeted towards her. Criticism is too painful, whether constructive or not. Putting herself down becomes a defence and a crutch.

Sister Put-Down does not realise that this type of behaviour is a subtle form of manipulation. Her reasoning is either:

- I'll verbally 'bash' myself before you do – because I can cope with my own bashing; or,
- Please disagree with me and praise me instead.

Is this you? _____

8. Sister 'People-Pleaser'

'Sister People-Pleaser' will go to desperate lengths to win the approval of others, because her sense of identity is primarily based on the assessment of others. Her values often change depending on what other people think or feel about any given topic.

Sister People-Pleaser lacks a strong sense of self; others can easily influence her, and she finds decision-making difficult.

Is this you? _____

9. Sister 'Introvert'

'Sister Introvert' is a timid person who is afraid of failure and rejection. Sister Introvert chooses to be alone rather than face rejection from others. She convinces herself that this is how it is meant to be. She is shy and gets embarrassed easily. Sister Introvert doesn't say much for fear of saying the wrong thing.

In your opinion, what do you think is going on here?

Is this you? _____

10. Sister 'Extrovert'

Although the life and soul of the party, **'Sister Introvert'** can often feel very lonely. She compensates for feelings of insecurity with her gift of delightful and engaging conversation. She doesn't have many friends but has lot of acquaintances. You will not find Sister Extrovert sitting at home, because she just cannot get enough of church activities. Her conversation is primarily superfi cial, and if asked how she is feeling, her response is usually, "I'm blessed and highly favoured," while inside she feels lonely and distant from others.

Is this you? _____

Now that you have had time to read through the descriptions, which of these 'masks' describe you?

Reflection Notes:

....

....

....

....

....

....

....

Exercise 4

Personal Reflection:

In pairs, explore questions 1-5
(please share your time equally) – 20 mins

1. With whom do you wear a mask?

_____

_____

_____

_____

2. Why do you wear a mask with this person/these people?

_____

_____

_____

_____

3. Can you recollect when you first began wearing a mask
    with this individual/group/fellowship? What was
    happening in your life?

_____

_____

_____

_____

Prayerfully reflect on this…

"And when thou prayest, thou shalt not be as the hypocrites are: for they love to pray standing in the synagogues and in the corners of the streets, that they may be seen of men."
Matthew 6:5 (KJV)

4. Do you wear a mask with Abba Father? In what way?

_____

_____

_____

_____

_____

_____

5. What are you afraid of Abba Father seeing? Do you know He sees all things (Proverbs 15:3)?

_____

_____

_____

_____

_____

_____

Exercise 5

⚠️ # Mask Activity (Part 1 & 2):

I give an '**self-care warning**' for this exercise, as it can bring up many buried emotions, so it is essential to exercise self-care. I encourage you to be truthful with your reflections, but if it all gets too much, say a prayer and go for a walk to ground yourself.

Activity 1 – Part 1: (10 minutes):

On your own, using the mask template below, write down keywords that demonstrate how you present yourself to Christ, others, your community, and the world.

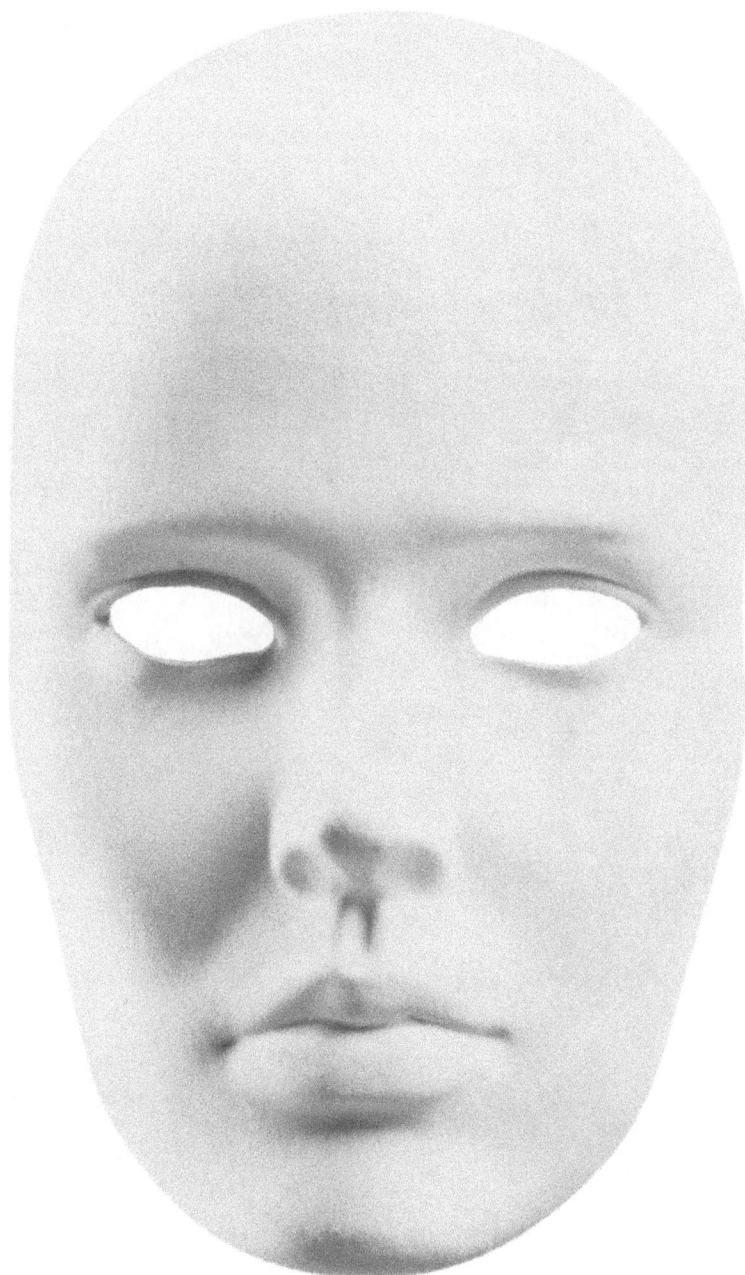

Exercise 6

Activity – Part 2: (10 mins)

Once you have completed your exterior mask, now use the mask template to write down keywords about how you really feel about yourself. For example, you may present at Church as being the 'martyr' but inside you lack self-esteem. When you have finished, share with your partner or a sister in Christ, allowing 10-15 minutes to share. **Keep to time boundaries!**

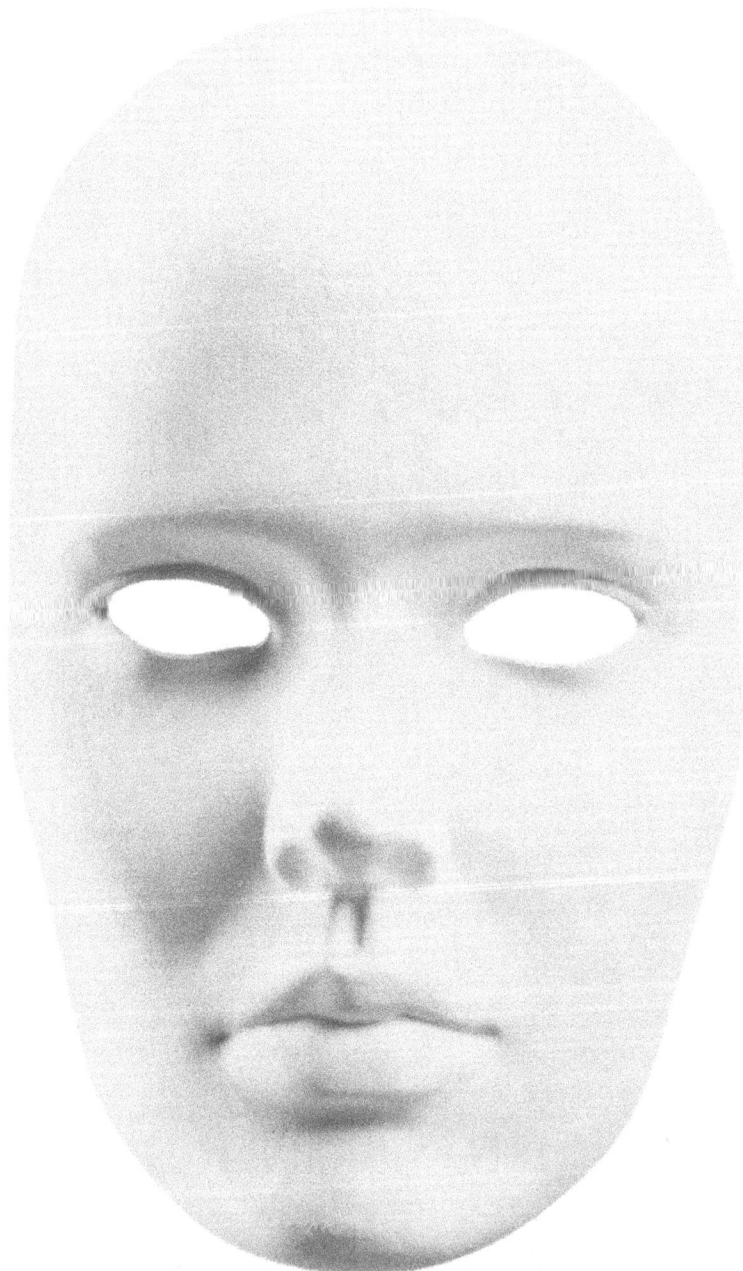

Call To Action

Dear Sister,

If you have managed to complete this chapter, well done. I can assure you that Christ is beginning His work in you and will see it through to its completion (Philippians 1:6). Amen!

You may not yet be a believer in Christ and have come across this book by divine appointment. You may be new to Christianity, and Christ is calling you to be a member of His worldwide family. You may be completing this workbook alone, or you may have been invited to join a Christian women's group to complete this workbook together. Whatever the reason, Christ wants to save you and redeem you from hell and eternity without him.

Maybe you are already a professed Christian, but your Christian Walk has gone cold or is lukewarm. Remember what scripture says about the lukewarm Christian? *"I will spue thee out of my mouth"* (Revelation 3:16 KJV).

If this describes you, it is not too late to invite/reinvite Christ Yeshua into your heart. To make Him your Lord and Saviour.

How might you do this?

Take your time and in a quiet space:

- Repent (express sincere regret or remorse about the sinful way you have lived).
- Ask Christ to forgive you and save you from the rightful penalty of eternal death (which you rightfully deserve).
- Confess with your mouth that 'Christ is Lord,' and believe with your heart that Yahweh raised Christ Yeshua from the dead (Romans 10:9).
- If you willingly surrender and say this prayer, asking Christ Yeshua into your heart, spirit, soul, and mind, scripture says, 'You will be saved!'

There is some amazing news I want to share with you once you have decided to be a follower of Christ Yeshua. Luke 15:10 (KJV) says, **"Likewise, I say unto you, there is joy in the presence of the angels of God over one sinner that repenteth."**

Sister in Christ, Heaven is rejoicing!

Homework 5

Spend time with Christ Yeshua in prayer and conversation.

- Share your feelings with Him about the masks you wear with Him and with others.
- Ask the Holy Spirit to show you where and when you began to wear a mask.
- Ask the Holy Spirit to show you how wearing such masks has allowed the enemy to have a foothold in your life.
- Ask the Holy Spirit to show you how this has led you into sinful behaviour.
- Repent of this behaviour and ask Abba Father for His forgiveness.
- Ask Abba Father to heal the broken places in your spirit, soul, and body that have been affected by the masks you wear.

END OF MODULE 5

Homework Reflections:

MODULE 6
DEALING WITH
UNGODLY ANGER

Module 6: Dealing with Ungodly Anger

"²⁶ Be ye angry, and sin not:
let not the sun go down upon your wrath:
²⁷ Neither give place to the devil."
Ephesians 4:26-27 (KJV)

Opening Prayer:

Group Contract:

If you are completing this programme within a group, I suggest you remind participants of the importance of adhering to and remaining committed to the group contract. Revisit the contract at the start of each session to ensure the group's safety. The group must adhere to it.

Session Aims

Explore our feelings and responses to our own righteous and unrighteous anger.

Session Outcomes

By the end of the session, delegates will be able to:

- Recognise the difference between **righteous** and **unrighteous anger.**
- Identify how 'anger' has impacted your life and walk as a daughter in Christ.
- Name three or more ways 'anger' has prevented you from walking in your heavenly calling.
- Identify areas of unhealed pain related to suppressing anger.
- Explore areas of righteous and unrighteous anger, and how it has prevented you from experiencing full deliverance and the healing power of Yahweh's love.

Session 6: This week we will be exploring - 'Dealing with Ungodly Anger'.

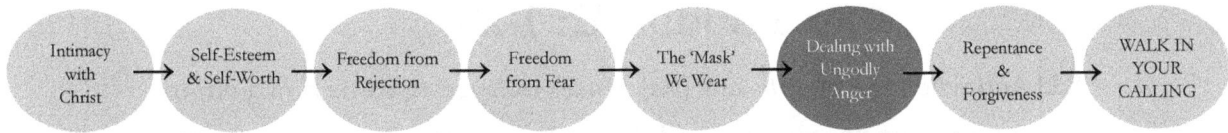

Intimacy with Christ → Self-Esteem & Self-Worth → Freedom from Rejection → Freedom from Fear → The 'Mask' We Wear → Dealing with Ungodly Anger → Repentance & Forgiveness → WALK IN YOUR CALLING

Check-in (10mins)

Delegates will share insights and reflections from session 5.

- If working as a group, set aside 15 minutes to share your learning about the masks your wear with Christ and others.
- **Please keep to time boundaries.**

Scripture Reading

Exodus 32: 1-20

"*32 And when the people saw that Moses delayed to come down out of
the mount, the people gathered themselves together unto Aaron, and
said unto him, Up, make us gods, which shall go before us; for as for this Moses,
the man that brought us up out of the land of Egypt,
we wot not what is become of him.*

*2 And Aaron said unto them, Break off the golden earrings,
which are in the ears of your wives, of your sons, and of your daughters,
and bring them unto me.*

*3 And all the people brake off the golden earrings which were in their ears,
and brought them unto Aaron.*

*4 And he received them at their hand, and fashioned it with a graving tool,
after he had made it a molten calf: and they said, These be thy gods,
O Israel, which brought thee up out of the land of Egypt.*

*5 And when Aaron saw it, he built an altar before it; and Aaron made
proclamation, and said, Tomorrow is a feast to the Lord.*

*6 And they rose up early on the morrow, and offered burnt offerings,
and brought peace offerings; and the people sat down to
eat and to drink, and rose up to play.*

*7 And the Lord said unto Moses, Go, get thee down; for thy people,
which thou broughtest out of the land of Egypt, have corrupted themselves:*

*8 They have turned aside quickly out of the way which I commanded them:
they have made them a molten calf, and have worshipped it,
and have sacrificed thereunto, and said, These be thy gods,
O Israel, which have brought thee up out of the land of Egypt.*

*9 And the Lord said unto Moses, I have seen this people,
and, behold, it is a stiffnecked people:*

*10 Now therefore let me alone, that my wrath may wax hot against them, and that I may
consume them: and I will make of thee a great nation.*

*11 And Moses besought the Lord his God, and said, Lord, why
doth thy wrath wax hot against thy people, which thou hast brought forth
out of the land of Egypt with great power, and with a mighty hand?*

^{12} *Wherefore should the Egyptians speak, and say, For mischief did he bring them out, to slay them in the mountains, and to consume them from the face of the earth? Turn from thy fierce wrath, and repent of this evil against thy people.*

^{13} *Remember Abraham, Isaac, and Israel, thy servants, to whom thou swarest by thine own self, and saidst unto them, I will multiply your seed as the stars of heaven, and all this land that I have spoken of will I give unto your seed, and they shall inherit it for ever.*

^{14} *And the Lord repented of the evil which he thought to do unto his people.*

^{15} *And Moses turned, and went down from the mount, and the two tables of the testimony were in his hand: the tables were written on both their sides; on the one side and on the other were they written.*

^{16} *And the tables were the work of God, and the writing was the writing of God, graven upon the tables.*

^{17} *And when Joshua heard the noise of the people as they shouted, he said unto Moses, There is a noise of war in the camp.*

^{18} *And he said, It is not the voice of them that shout for mastery, neither is it the voice of them that cry for being overcome: but the noise of them that sing do I hear.*

^{19} *And it came to pass, as soon as he came nigh unto the camp, that he saw the calf, and the dancing: and Moses' anger waxed hot, and he cast the tables out of his hands, and brake them beneath the mount.*

^{20} *And he took the calf which they had made, and burnt it in the fire, and ground it to powder, and strawed it upon the water, and made the children of Israel drink of it."*

Personal Reflection Point:

Exercise 1

On your own, in pairs/threes:

- How does this piece of scripture speak to you about the nature and expression of anger?
- **Write your reflections below:**

....

....

....

....

What is 'Anger'?

In this module, we will look at how we express and manage anger. We will also explore what is meant by 'righteous' and 'unrighteous' anger.

Hebrew Definition of the word 'Anger'

The Hebrew word 'naphiym' is associated with the word 'nose', or 'nostrils' when written in the plural form, but it can also mean 'anger'. If we are really very angry, our nostrils can flare. A literal interpretation of Jonathan's physical presentation of anger in 1 Samuel 20:34 is interpreted in Hebrew as a 'burning nose' or 'fierce anger'.

When we feel angry:

We can experience irritability, tightness in the chest, feelings of nausea, palpitations, to name but a few emotional responses.

Exercise 2

How do we handle anger?

In pairs/threes, spend 15 minutes designing a quick mind map of how **you** handle anger concerning the following categories of people/entities:

- Your home nation
- Your husband
- Your family
- Your fellowship
- Your place of work
- Your communities
- The Government
- With Abba Father

Can you think of anymore?

- _____
- _____
- _____

Use the notes page to write your reflections. Try to notice any patterns or insights. Be prepared to share with the group or a sister in Christ.

Notes:

What makes ME angry?

Anger has been described as the most difficult emotion to handle. It is often the primary cause of relationship breakups. People live with regret over words spoken in anger. These harmful words said in anger can cause lasting harm to us, to people, communities, and nations.

Anger is a human emotion that we all experience at various times in our lives. Anger can vary in intensity from mild irritation to rage. However, to understand anger, we first need to understand ourselves. We need to explore and understand our anger and the root of it.

Exercise 3:

In pairs/threes (five minutes each to share)

Discuss in pairs/threes, what you have been taught about the expression of anger?

Notes:_____

_____

_____

_____

_____

_____

_____

_____

_____

Anger is...

Anger can be a good thing. Anger can spur us on to make the necessary changes in our lives. Anger (if expressed in a righteous way), can give us a way to express negative feelings or motivate us to find solutions to problems.

Exercise 4

Understanding Anger

Have you ever wondered why you are angry? Briefly write some keywords of how you manage each of the situations below. Think of examples to support your responses. Exploring these situations can help us to identify the (perceived or actual) root causes of anger:

- **Frustration – How do you deal with this? (anger at others, e.g. pastors, parents, caregivers, at ourselves, etc.). 1 Kings 21:1-16**

Personal Example: _____
_____

- **Failure – others, self, towards Yahweh. 2 Kings 5: 11-12**

Personal Example: _____
_____

- **Rejection – from family, people, communities, church family. 1 Samuel 8:7**

Personal Example: _____
_____

- **Injustice – unfair behaviour at home, family, school, communities. 2 Samuel 12:1-7**

Personal Example: _____
_____

- **Betrayal – divorce, adultery. Genesis 34:1–7**

Personal Example:_____
_____

- **Insults to our values. 1 Peter 4:4**

Personal Example: _____
_____

- **Unhealed hurts – Past hurtful experiences by people we care for or have some regard for us. Psalm 38:7**

Personal Example: _____
_____

- **Ungodly generational iniquity. Genesis 3**

Personal Example:_____
_____

- **Demonic influences. Genesis 4: 6-7**

Personal Example: _____
_____

- **Responses to fear. 1 Kings 19:3**

Personal Example: _____
_____

- **Observing examples of ungodly anger as a child (domestic violence/abuse).**

Personal Example: _____
_____

Exercise 5

Personal Reflection Point:

- How did you express anger when growing up?
- What did you learn about how you expressed anger/or not?
- What have you learned about the impact of your expression of anger, i.e., how does it affect you and others?

Reflections: _____

_____

_____

_____

_____

_____

_____

_____

_____

_____

_____

_____

_____

_____

_____

_____

_____

_____

_____

_____

Another Scripture Reference...

Our Father in Heaven gets angry when his people sin and are unrighteous in their behaviours.

There are over 700 references to anger demonstrated in different ways in the Bible. On page 128, we see how the word 'anger' is defined in the Hebrew dictionary. Let's have a look at another scripture reference.

Isaiah 13:9 (KJV)

"Behold, the day of the LORD cometh, cruel both with wrath and fierce anger, to lay the land desolate: and he shall destroy the sinners thereof out of it."

Then we have **fierce** anger. The word for fierce is **'ebrah',** which comes from the root word **'ebar',** and in its Semitic root it is a word used when a river overflows its banks. When anger is out of control, it may feel like a river has overflowed its banks.

The word 'anger' in Hebrew is also not clearly defined. It is the word 'aneph'. It means to snort. It comes from the snorting of a camel. Camels may snort when forced to do something they do not want to do. A camel will also snort in grief if its mate or calf dies, and when it is in heat and desires intimacy. **Can you think of any biblical references that describe Yahweh's flaring nostrils?**

Sometimes, we are raised to believe that Yahweh is continually angry with us and that His sole purpose is to punish or chastise us. However, from Genesis to Revelation, we see Yahweh's determination to rescue His people – where is the 'anger' in this? The Bible is a a love story, a story of redemption.

In Isaiah 13:9, Yahweh is willing to destroy the land so that His people will return to Him and turn from their wicked and idolatrous ways. That sounds like love because He wants to continue to bless His people and fulfil His covenant with them.

Knowing that fear can operate behind a spirit of anger is essential.

Greek Interpretation of 'Anger'…

There are two words to describe 'anger' in the Bible. These are:

- Orge
- Thumos

Orgē (ὀργή) comes from the verb oragō, meaning 'to swell', and can imply a sudden outburst. But when referring to God's anger, the word can be defined as 'fixed', 'controlled' and 'passionate feeling against sin' (see 1 Thessalonians 1:10).

Words and phrases associated with the word 'orge' are: anger, temper, agitation of the soul, impulse, desire, and any violent emotion. But especially anger, wrath, and indignation, exhibited in punishment – hence used for punishment itself.

Thumos (θυμός – also commonly spelt 'thymos') is a Greek word expressing the concept of being active, alive, and vigorous. There is also a physical association with this word, with its association to breath or blood.

The anger of Yahweh

Biblical references show Yahweh being very angry at sin and unrighteousness in individuals, groups of people, and nations (Genesis 18:30 and 32, Numbers 22:22 and 25:2-59).

Below are just some of the reasons why Yahweh showed his anger:

- Idolatry, Deuteronomy 6:14 to 15, and 28 and 29; and Disobedience, Joshua 7:1.

  1. **Can you find any other scripture references to Yehovah's anger?**
  2. **Can you find any New Testament scripture references to Christ's anger?**

The Wrath of Yahweh...

Yahweh's anger results in judgment and punishment (Deuteronomy 29:22-29).

Every spirit-filled Christian must be aware that **we are saved from the wrath of God through the sacrifice of Christ Yeshua.**

Scriptural examples of anger:

Old Testament:

- The first mention of anger in the Scriptures refers to Cain – Genesis 4: 1–10.
- In the Book of Exodus, there are several examples of Yahweh's anger towards his people when they are disobedient.
- The sin of David and Bathsheba – David and Nathan, 2 Samuel 12:5.

New Testament:

- Yeshua becomes very angry about the buying and selling taking place within the temple courts – Matthew 21:12-13.
- Christ responding to the attitude of the Jewish leaders (Pharisees and Sadducees) – Mark 3:5
- Christ's great displeasure at his disciples – Mark 10:14.
- Jesus becomes angry with an unclean spirit of infirmity – Mark 1:41.

Yahweh's Guidance

- The warning is to be slow to anger, for a foolish man lives on anger – Proverbs 12:16.
- Anger eventually results in its punishment and more strife and contention, ill health, and sometimes death – Proverbs 19:19.
- Harsh words stir up anger; hence, it is advisable not to associate yourself with angry people – Proverbs 15:1; 22:24.
- Do not respond in anger and seek to live in peace with our brothers and sisters – Colossians 3:8.
- Christ left us with His peace, a 'shalom' peace in this fallen world, a peace that cannot be understood by those not in Christ, so take advantage of it. It is free – John 14:27.

Can you think of any more Bible references?

What's Lies Beneath The ANGER?

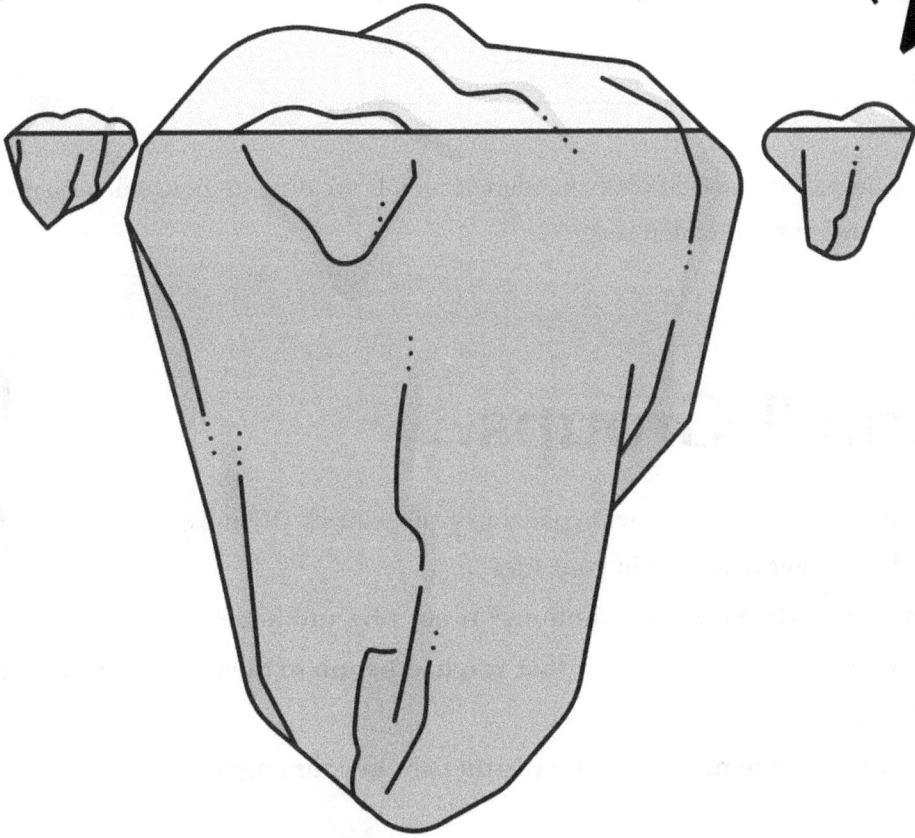

When we become angry, it can become a dangerous environment. How we respond must not open the door to sin and cause destruction in our lives and the lives of others (Ephesians 4:26-32). We must deal with our anger in a godly way, seeking to identify the root cause, taking responsibility for our responses, and not letting bitterness grow.

Exercise 6

Group Discussion

Consider the following question:

What types of feelings can be masked as anger? (10mins)

1._____

2._____

3._____

4._____

5._____

We must recognise if we have difficulty handling anger. If we do not, there will be signs and symptoms that will bring attention to it.

Exercise 7

In Small Groups...

Discuss the following questions – be prepared to give feedback (10 mins):

1. How does anger manifest in your life?

2. Do you regularly bury your emotions? If so, why and how?

3. Can you pinpoint when you felt that you had begun to bury your emotions rather than express them?

4. How can you be honest with Abba Father about your anger?

Reflections: _____

_____

_____

_____

_____

Exercise 8

Anger Questionnaire

If you are finding it difficult to be honest with your anger, try this short quiz below.

Tick all that apply:

1. I find it difficult to forgive those who have hurt me. _____
2. I easily become defensive when confronted. _____
3. My voice needs to be louder in an argument. _____
4. At times I can't control the urge to hit another person. _____
5. I find it hard to forget the pain people have caused me. _____
6. I seek to control the conversation when I feel I am losing an argument. _____
7. I describe my angry behaviour as 'passionate'. _____
8. I have trouble controlling my temper. _____
9. I often criticise and judge others who have hurt me. _____
10. I can explode at the slightest issue without warning. _____
11. I avoid confrontation with others. _____
12. I allow others to express their anger for me. _____
13. I tend to withdraw into my 'shell' when angry. _____
14. I often try to convince others that "I don't get angry." _____
15. I feel inwardly hurt if people do not address my needs. _____
16. I avoid people I who challenge me. _____
17. I continually replay my injustices over and over in my mind. _____
18. I continually share (with anyone who will listen) to the negative things that have happened to me in my life. _____
19. I have difficulty accepting Yahweh's blessings. _____
20. I often wonder why I feel so bitter about things. _____
21. I feel my family and friends take every opportunity to put me down. _____
22. I am quick to start an argument. _____
23. I can act verbally and physically violent to others, slam doors, throw things, shout at people, and use disrespectful language when I am upset. _____
24. I become passive-aggressive when people do not agree with me. _____
25. I have a right to express anger whenever I like in whatever way I like. _____

TOTAL ✔ out of 25: _____

Look at each question's theme for which you scored highly. What is it telling you about how you manage/express anger? Where did you learn to express anger in this way?

How do you handle anger from the past?

Please tick the appropriate statement and reflect on your answers:

- ☐ Denial and burial.
- ☐ Avoid or ignore.
- ☐ Store up my anger.
- ☐ Spurts out and I get angry at the small issues.
- ☐ I feel depressed – a result of anger turned in on oneself.

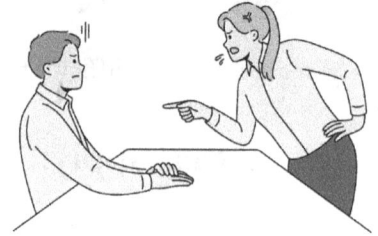

Do you have a problem with anger?

Our current attitude and behaviours may indicate we have difficulty with the management of our anger, such as:

1. **Self-blame** – this can result in self-harm, anger towards Yahweh and against everybody, etc.
2. **Suppression and control of anger to protect oneself** – can be unplanned and uncontrolled disruptions in anger when others are least expecting it.
3. **Criticism** – towards others and self.
4. **Aggressiveness and/or hostility** – violence towards self, others, or property.
5. **Blaming others** – not willing to take responsibility for your part. Being a victim.
6. **Confrontation** – reactionary, rather than being still and waiting on Yahweh for guidance.
7. **Over Thinking** – going round and round over the same issues and refusing to release your pain to Christ.
8. **Frustration** – against others, things, or oneself.
9. **Perfectionism** – the need to control self and others.
10. **Depression** – can be an indicator of not releasing anger in a godly way.

From the list above, what is your 'go-to' response to managing anger?

It is essential that you take responsibility for sinful attitudes and responses to anger, and deal with any anger you are holding.

Exercise 9

Please use the next page to respond to the questions below:

- In pairs (10 minutes each), share your findings. What did you learn? Can you link the way you respond to anger to a specific incident or experience?
- How did your caregivers respond to your anger?
- Were you shut down or allowed to express your anger? Were your caregivers the only ones allowed to express anger?

Anger…
My response…

Exercise 10

Who Am I Angry With? (10 mins)

Consider the following list of key people you may be angry with. Please state specifically, why you are angry with them:

Yahweh: ....

Christ Yeshua: ....

The Holy Spirit: ....

Satan: ....

Adam: ....

Eve: ....

Me: ....

Family: ....

Friends: ....

Teachers: ....

Employers: ....

Institutions: ....

Health Care Insitutions: ....

GP: ....

The World: ....

Others: ....

....

Reflect honestly on your anger and reasons for feeling this way; write about it in your journal. Please see your homework templates from page 210 onwards to help you further explore your responses to anger.

Righteous Anger...

We cannot leave this section of this workbook without talking about **'righteous anger'**. Understanding this phrase will help you to understand if you have a right before Yahweh to be angry.

To understand this, let us look briefly at Matthew 21: 12-13 (KJV),

> "*12 And Jesus went into the temple of God, and cast out all them that sold and bought in the temple, and overthrew the tables of the moneychangers, and the seats of them that sold doves,*
> *13 And said unto them, It is written, My house shall be called the house of prayer; but ye have made it a den of thieves.*"

Exercise 11

Group Discussion...

- Why was Yeshua angry?
- What right did Yeshua have to be angry with the Jews concerning what was going on in the temple?
- How might you have responded?
- Do you agree with Christ's actions?

Furthermore, Christ acknowledges that as humans (spirit, soul, and body), we will experience anger but must follow Christ's guidance. Please read Ephesians 4:26.

- What do you sense Christ is trying to communicate to the believer?

Steps to Godly Expression of Anger...

Exercise 12

Without looking at page 145, reflect on the following question?

- **How can I safely express my anger to prevent me from sinning? List as many ways that you can safely express your anger. The first one is done for you:**

How can I express my anger in a healthy way?

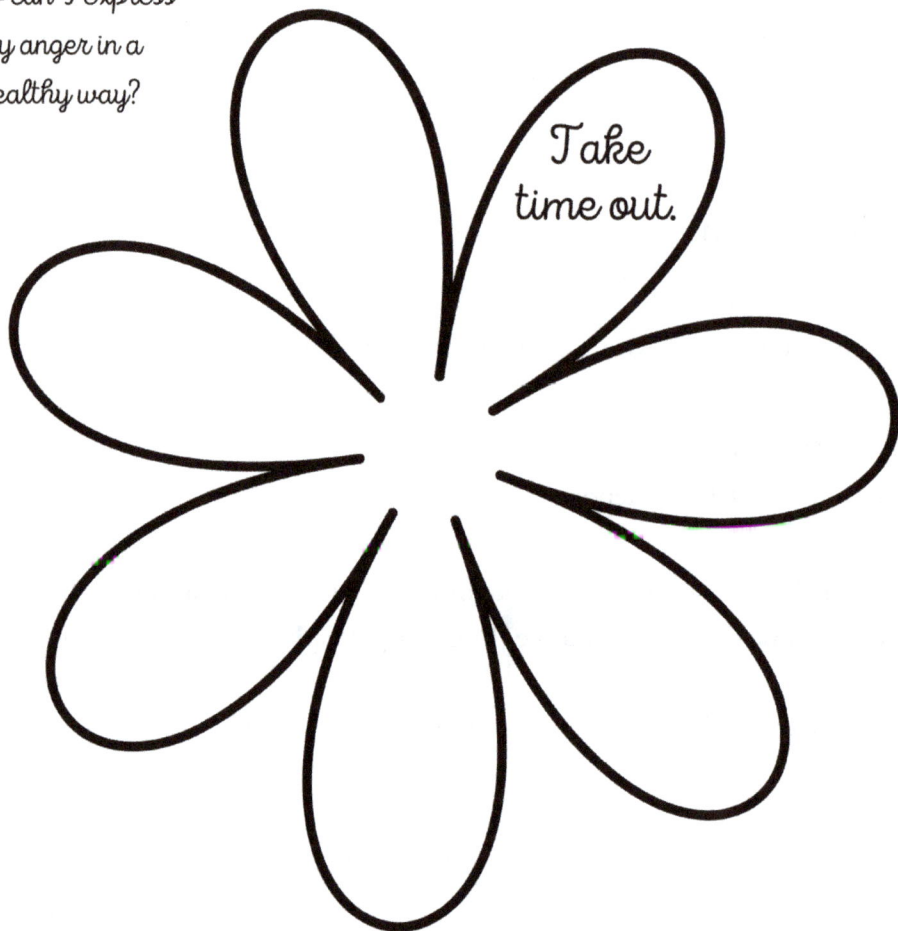

Take time out.

Let's now look at how Christ says we should deal with our anger.

How can you safely express your anger to prevent you from sinning?

- Admit you are angry and take responsibility.
- Admit how you feel – name your feelings of anger, etc; connect with your anger and its roots.
- Be truthful about what you have gained from remaining angry – some of us like remining angry as it gives us a sense of purpose.
- Repent of any sinful behaviour.
- Experience the pain you feel because of your anger (you may need a box of tissues).
- Seek to forgive self and others (we will tackle this again in Lesson 7).
- Fast and pray for Yahweh to remove the 'spirit of anger' from your life, if you find that you are still angry.

You can practise this by sharing a situation you are currently angry about.
Only spend 10 minutes sharing your example.

So, what are godly expressions of anger?

- Recognising that anger does evaporate into thin air.
- Recognising that anger will eventually find a way of being expressed, no matter how much you try to suppress it (it's a bit like a leak).
- Asking Abba Father to help you express anger in godly way.
- Asking Abba to show you the root of where your anger lies.
- Identifying ways you might comfortably release your anger.
- Using the iceberg template on page 216 to help you to identify the root causes.

Exercise 13

The following suggestions might be useful. Please note your expression of anger must not cause harm to you, your property, or anyone else's.

- ☐ Pouring out your heart to Christ Yeshua
- ☐ Prayer
- ☐ Wise counsel with a Pastor, Prayer Sister, Christian counsellor, etc.
- ☐ Shouting into the air (not at someone else)
- ☐ Talking to a friend
- ☐ Worship and Praise
- ☐ Gardening
- ☐ Dancing
- ☐ Listening to Christian music
- ☐ Journaling or creative writing
- ☐ Cleaning
- ☐ **Anymore?**..

....

It is still important to explore the root of your anger with Christ.
Ask the Holy Spirit to show you any unhealed areas of your life.
Continue to pray for healing.

FINAL THOUGHTS...

When continually angry, we do not give the Holy Spirit room to heal us. When we are continually angry, people avoid us. We often think that people cannot see or experience our anger, but they can.

Christ described the Holy Spirit as the "Comforter" (2 Corinthians 1:3-4) who heals and transforms us to be like Christ. Therefore, resisting ungodly anger is essential to avoid giving the enemy a foothold (Ephesians 4:27).

Seek to be continually filled with the Holy Spirit. The Bible says we are a temple for the Holy Spirit.

"¹⁹ What? know ye not that your body is the temple of the Holy Ghost, which is in you, which ye have of God, and ye are not your own? ²⁰ For ye are bought with a price: therefore glorify God in your body, and in your spirit, which are God's."

1 Corinthians 6:19-20 (KJV)

If we believe in the above, how can ungodly anger continue to reside in us? Reflect on this piece of scripture. Scripture demonstrates the importance of keeping our 'house' clean, (spirit, soul, mind, and body). We need to be continually overflowing with the Holy Spirit (Ruach HaKodesh). The consequences of not doing this can be found in Matthew:

" ⁴³ When the unclean spirit is gone out of a man, he walketh through dry places, seeking rest, and findeth none. ⁴⁴ Then he saith, I will return into my house from whence I came out; and when he is come, he findeth it empty, swept, and garnished. ⁴⁵ Then goeth he, and taketh with himself seven other spirits more wicked than himself, and they enter in and dwell there: and the last state of that man is worse than the first. Even so shall it be also unto this wicked generation."
Matthew 12:43-45 (KJV)

Call To Action!

Dear Sister,

If you have managed to complete this chapter, well done. I can assure you that Christ is beginning His work in you and will see it through to its completion. Amen.

You may not be a believer in Christ, but you may have either come across the book by divine appointment and may be completing this workbook alone, or you may have been invited to join a Christian women's group to complete this workbook together. Maybe you are new to Christianity. Whatever the reason, Christ Yeshua is calling you to be a member of His worldwide family. He wants to save you and redeem you from hell and eternity without Him.

Maybe you are already a professed Christian, but your Christian Walk has gone cold or lukewarm. Remember what scripture says about the lukewarm Christian? Revelation 3:16 (KJV) says, *"I will spue thee out of my mouth."*

If this describes you, it is not too late to invite/reinvite Christ Yeshua into your heart and to commit to making Christ the Lord and Saviour of your life.

How might you do this?

Take your time, and in a quiet space:

- Repent (express sincere regret or remorse about your sinful life).
- Ask Christ to forgive you and save you from the rightful penalty of eternal death (which you rightfully deserve).
- Confess with your mouth that Christ is Lord! Believe with your heart that Yahweh raised Christ Yeshua from the dead.
- If you willingly surrender and say this prayer, asking Christ Yeshua into your heart, spirit, soul, and mind, scripture says, 'You will be saved!'

Let me also share this amazing scripture with you now that you have decided to follow Christ Yeshua. Luke 15:10 (KJV) says, **_"Likewise, I say unto you, there is joy in the presence of the angels of God over one sinner that repenteth."_**

Sister in Christ, Heaven is rejoicing!

Homework 6

"Be ye angry, and sin not: let not the sun go down upon your wrath."
Ephesians 4:26 (KJV)

- Pray and seek Christ's guidance and protection as you do this work as you seek deliverance from the 'spirit of anger'.

- Prayerfully complete (if you have not done so already) the anger list and questions associated with it on page 150.

- **Creative work:** Make time to be alone with Abba Father. Ask the Holy Spirit to show you what your anger looks like to Abba Father.

- Begin to talk to Abba Father about how anger is affecting your life.

- Ask Abba Father to show you who you need to forgive for their displays of ungodly anger towards you – this may be generational.

- Ask Abba Father to show you your displays of ungodly anger towards others.

- Seek to truly repent of this behaviour.

- Write a letter to Christ Yeshua concerning your anger (be detailed, Christ can handle your anger).

- **Classwork Discussion:** In preparation for next week's lesson, read the story of Tamar (Genesis 38) and the catastrophic events resulting from anger amongst her brothers.

- **Please feel free to share your reflections in the group, or with a sister in Christ if you are completing this programme alone.**

END OF WORKBOOK 6

Homework 1 – Anger List

Prayerfully ask the Holy Spirit to show you who you are still angry with and write them out in the boxes below. Once you have completed this sheet, move on to completing Exercise 2.

No.	Family/Loved ones	Friends/Church Family	Colleagues	Organisations (school, employers, hospitals, etc.)
1.				
2.				
3.				
4.				
5.				
6.				
7.				
8.				
9.				
10.				
11.				
12.				
13.				
14.				
15.				
16.				
17.				
18.				
19.				
20.				
21.				
22.				
23.				
24.				

Homework 2 – Anger List – Exploration

You can photocopy this exercise for everyone you have identified on your Anger List on page 150. Make sure to include this vital part. These questions will get to the root of your anger. Ask the Holy Spirit to guide you.

Once you have completed this sheet, write your heartfelt letter to Christ Yeshua. The template can be found on page 222.

Copy this template as many times as you need to.

1. Who are you angry with?...................................... (one person/institution etc.)

2. The situation/person/organisation, etc., I am angry about is (Write in as much detail as you can.):

....

....

....

....

....

....

3. How did you feel about what Yahweh/person/church/organisation did to you? (Again, be very explicit and honest with how you have felt/feel.)

....

....

....

....

....

....

4. How have you responded to your anger, i.e. in a righteous or unrighteous way? Give explicit examples of this. Examples of this could be unforgiveness, being critical of others, jealousy, etc.

....

....

....

....

....

....

5. Consider whether this response has helped or hindered you. Say how.

....

....

....

....

....

....

6. Has there been a pattern to your anger, i.e. angry with your father, and hence you are angry with all men and/or people in authority? Again, reflect on how this has impacted your life.

....

....

....

....

....

7. Write a note/letter prayerfully, honestly and openly to Christ Yeshua. Share from your heart how you feel you deserved/deserve to be treated (righteous anger). Remember, Christ is our intercessor. He will reveal Abba's heart to you.

In your letter, repent of any ungodly responses to this anger (we will deal with this in module 7). Again, be explicit with how you responded to the situation.

Dear Christ Yeshua,

MODULE 7
REPENTANCE
& FORGIVENESS

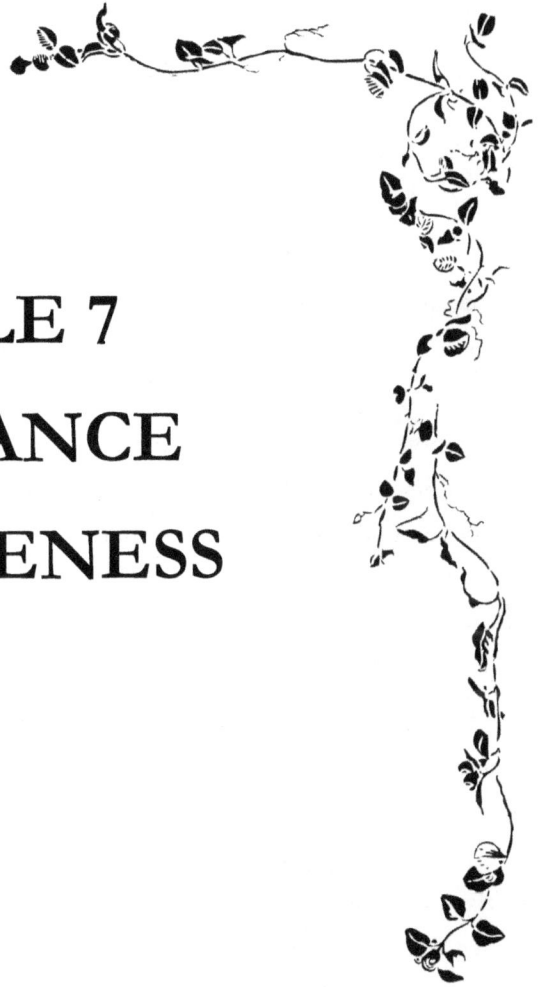

Heart Warning...

Dear Sister in Christ,

Over the past few weeks/months, we have embarked on this journey in Christ – a journey I hope has begun to transform you, enabling you to fulfil your amazing destiny as a Daughter of the King of kings.

Throughout this workbook, you have explored themes of rejection, self-esteem, and anger, among many other topics. There is no doubt that this workbook could have tackled so many more conditions of the heart. The Bible tells us, "there is no new thing under the sun" (Ecclesiastes 1:9).

Experiencing pain, sorrow, loss, and rejection, amongst other painful heart conditions, is not new.

The exercises in this book may have revealed areas in your life that remain unhealed. People, places, organisations, or businesses may have been attached to these painful memories or experiences, so in this chapter I encourage you **not** to overlook or minimise these important exercises on repentance and forgiveness. If you must, keep returning to the exercises again and again. Our Lord wants you whole!

You may have hidden your hurts away in the attic of your mind, hoping they will cease to exist. I need to tell you they will never go away unless you allow Christ and the Holy Spirit in to clear up the mess. Remember what Christ said to His apostles when He gave instructions on how to pray,

> "14 **For if ye forgive men their trespasses, your heavenly**
> **Father will also forgive you:**
>
> 15 **But if ye forgive not men their trespasses,**
> **neither will your Father forgive your trespasses.**"
> *Matthew 6:14 (KJV)*

We are commanded (yes, commanded) to forgive others. It is the only way Abba Father can forgive us of our sins. There is an action and a reaction within the act of true forgiveness, but there is something more; Christ promises us release from the 'unforgiveness prison' and promises a more fulfilling relationship with the Father, Son, and the Holy Spirit. So please do not worry if you get stuck and feel resistant. Put the workbook down, pray, fast and return when you can. Abba Father wants to free His Daughters so they can live a life with a 'peace of God, which passeth all understanding.' (Philippians 4:7 KJV).

Module 7: Repentance & Forgiveness

"If we confess our sins, He is faithful and just to forgive us our sins, and to cleanse us from all unrighteousness."
1 John1:9 (KJV)

Opening Prayer:

Group Contract:

If you are completing this programme within a group, please remind group members of the importance of adhering to and remaining committed to the group contract. Always revisit the contract at the start of each session to ensure the group's safety. The group must adhere to it. If you need to, pin your group contract to the wall where all can see it.

Session Aims

Understand the meaning, impact, and importance of true repentance and forgiveness.

Outcomes

By the end of the session, delegates will be able to:

- Explain what repentance is and is not.
- Explain what forgiveness is and is not.
- Name three or more ways 'unforgiveness' has held you captive.
- Identify how unrepentance and unforgiveness have impacted your relationship with Abba Father and others.
- Identify areas of unforgiveness towards others and self.

Session 7: In this module, we will explore: 'Repentance & Forgiveness'

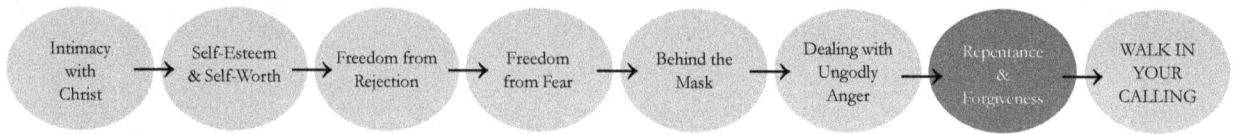

Check-in (10mins)

Delegates will share insights and reflections from session 6.

- If working as a group, set aside 15-30 minutes to share your five-minute 'Anger' reflections from Module 6 and your reflections on the story of Tamar in Genesis 38.
- **Please keep to time boundaries.**

Scripture Reading

Matthew 18: 21-35 (KJV)

"²¹ Then came Peter to him, and said, Lord, how oft shall
my brother sin against me, and I forgive him? till seven times?
²² Jesus saith unto him, I say not unto thee, Until seven times: but,
Until seventy times seven.
²³ Therefore is the kingdom of heaven likened unto a certain king,
which would take account of his servants. ²⁴ And when he had begun to reckon,
one was brought unto him, which owed him ten thousand talents.
²⁵ But forasmuch as he had not to pay, his lord commanded him to be sold,
and his wife, and children, and all that he had, and payment to be made.
²⁶ The servant therefore fell down, and worshipped him, saying,
Lord, have patience with me, and I will pay thee all.
²⁷ Then the lord of that servant was moved with compassion,
and loosed him, and forgave him the debt.
²⁸ But the same servant went out, and found one of his fellowservants,
which owed him an hundred pence: and he laid hands on him,
and took him by the throat, saying, Pay me that thou owest.
²⁹ And his fellowservant fell down at his feet, and besought him,
saying, Have patience with me, and I will pay thee all.
³⁰ And he would not: but went and cast him into prison,
till he should pay the debt.
³¹ So when his fellowservants saw what was done, they were very sorry,
and came and told unto their lord all that was done.
³² Then his lord, after that he had called him, said unto him,
O thou wicked servant, I forgave thee all that debt,
because thou desiredst me:
³³ Shouldest not thou also have had compassion on thy fellowservant,
even as I had pity on thee?
³⁴ And his lord was wroth, and delivered him to the tormentors,
till he should pay all that was due unto him.
³⁵ So likewise shall my heavenly Father do also unto you,
if ye from your hearts forgive not every one his brother their trespasses."

Exercise 1

Forgiveness

Group Discussion... (15 mins)

1. **How does this chapter in Scripture talk about the nature of forgiveness?**
2. Reflect on the consequences of unforgiveness for Yahweh's children.
3. Reflect on Yahweh's mercy towards us when we repent of our own unforgiveness.
4. **Write your reflections below and be prepared to share them with your group or a sister in Christ.**

Reflections:

_____

_____

_____

_____

_____

_____

_____

_____

_____

_____

_____

Christ's Response:

1. **What is Christ communicating through this parable?**
2. **What does true repentance and forgiveness look like?**
3. **How does Abba Father respond?**

Consider the magnitude of the servant's debt...

How might the servant accumulate such a bill?

- The servant comes to the King, repenting and begging for forgiveness, because he knows his debt would mean imprisonment for him and all his family (generational curses).
- The King believes his cries for mercy and lets the servant go free.
- **Please note:** Where Christ Yeshua talks of ten thousand talents, this would be calculated as approximately 60 million denarii (today's value) or 60 million days of work. Wow!
- The pay for one day's work during this time was one denarii.
- Christ is trying to illustrate that our debt is so large that if He did not atone for our sin on the cross of Calvary, we too would spend eternity in hell.
- The servant is ecstatic when the King pardons him. He and his family are set free.
- We see in Matthew 18:28-30 that the servant suffered from short-term memory loss. He had forgotten that his own slate had been wiped clean by the King. He then had the audacity to harass another man and his family for the money they owed him! He showed no grace and sent debtor and his family to prison.
- But other servants of the King witnessed his hypocritical behaviour and promptly let the King know.
- There were consequences for the unmerciful servant due to his false repentance and lack of forgiveness for others (even though he was forgiven of his huge debt; a debt he could never repay).
- **The consequences:** At the command of the King, he was delivered to the torturers. He was imprisoned until he could pay back all his debt. For this man and his family, it would mean eternity (generational iniquity).

What do we learn?

- **Christ Yeshua called the servant to repent.** "If we confess our sins, He is faithful and just to forgive us our sins and to cleanse us from all unrighteousness" (1 John 1:9).
- Follow the instructions of the Lord's Prayer – it is a commandment.
- The Bible warns us that unforgiveness can lead to bitterness (Hebrews 12:15). Generational unforgiveness and repentance can cause endless problems, not only for us but also for loved ones, friends, and associates. Whole families, churches, and communities can be adversely

affected by unforgiveness.

- Unforgiveness can cause physical, mental, and spiritual pain, i.e. feeling tortured.

- Lastly, it will separate us from Christ, which will mean Yahweh will not listen to us. Christ is our intercessor. Christ said, ***"So likewise shall my heavenly Father do also unto you, if ye from your hearts forgive not everyone his brother their trespasses"*** (Matthew 18:35). We too will be thrown into a torturous prison of unforgiveness. Our sinful behaviour will separate us from the one who calls himself our "Healer".

- **Do you have any more insights you have gained from this piece of scripture? If yes, share them with the group or a sister in Christ.**

Forgiveness...

Definition of the word 'Forgiveness'

The biblical definition of 'forgiveness' is understood as:

- **Yahweh's promise not to count our sins against us.**

1 Corinthians 13:5 says when we forgive others, we give up the right to control the outcome and/or issue a judgement.

What is forgiveness?

Forgiveness is the decision to overcome the pain inflicted on us by another person. It means we are choosing to let go of anger, regret, resentment, shame, and other emotions associated with the injustices we have faced, even though our feelings might be entirely justified. In doing so, we are treating the offender with compassion, even though they are not entitled to it. Christ treats us with compassion daily, even though we do not deserve it.

For some of us, reconciliation with those who have hurt us or let us down may be possible, but in some cases reconciliation may put us in danger (danger is not what Christ wants for us). However, we are still commanded to forgive. We forget the injustice but do not condone or excuse the offender's behaviour. We choose to be merciful towards the offender and resist revenge. We can then be free to live our lives in the freedom of Christ.

What Forgiveness is?

1. **Our willingness to repent of our disobedience in not forgiving others, like our Father has forgiven us (Luke 23:34).**

2. **Our decision to repent and not hold onto unforgiveness against self and others, including Abba Father.**

3. **Our decision to allow Abba Father to heal the pain inflicted on us by another/ others.**

4. **Asking Abba Father to help you let go of anger, resentment, shame, and other emotions associated with an injustice, even though they are reasonable feelings.**

5. **Asking Abba Father to assist you in treating the offender with compassion (not easy), even though they are not entitled to it.**

6. **Forgetting the injustice, like Yahweh promises us (Isaiah 43.25 & Hebrews 10:17).**

What Forgiveness is not?

1. Reconciliation with the person that has hurt you or offended you, especially if they are still a danger to you and your loved ones. However, the Bible does ask us to work towards reconciliation if it is possible (Ephesians 4:31-32).

2. Condoning the offender's behaviour – Yahweh will avenge every wrongdoing (Hebrews 10:30). Asking Abba Father to assist you in treating the offender with compassion, (even though they are not entitled to it). Remember the offender does **not** need to be involved in this process. For example, we do not need to shout from the rooftops that we are willing to forgive. Our actions, our sense of peace and release will be evident to all.

3. 'Letting go' but secretly plotting revenge.

the Process of Forgiveness

You will now look at how the personal injustices you have endured in your lifetime have affected you. **On your own,** use the space below to write your reflections. Revisit your 'anger' list if needed.

Exercise 2: Make a list of all the injustices you have experienced. Just write bullet points, for example, 'My parents divorced when I was a baby.'

1. ....
2. ....
3. ....
4. ....
5. ....
6. ....
7. ....
8. ....
9. ....
10. ....
11. ....
12. ....
13. ....
14. ....
15. ....
16. ....
17. ....
18. ....
19. ....
20. ....

21. ....
22. ....
23. ....
24. ....
25. ....
26. ....
27. ....
19. ....
20. ....
21. ....
22. ....
23. ....
24. ....
25. ....
26. ....
27. ....
28. ....
29. ....
30. ....
31. ....
32. ....
33. ....
34. ....
35. ....
36. ....
37. ....
38. ....
39. ....

'Bring & Share' – Forgiveness Exercise

(10) For this part of this exercise, you must be specific and write the **name(s)** of those who have been unjust towards you, i.e. Uncle J, etc. I have divided them into categories to help you. Continue with a separate sheet if you need to. If in a group, take five minutes to complete this list on your own first. Once completed, share it with your peer. Share your reflections with your group or a sister in Christ. **In the interest of privacy, please do not write full names.**

Loved Ones

Brothers & Sisters

Place of Work/Study

Communities/ Nations/Others

Exercise 3

Unforgiveness can also affect the physical body, i.e. increased stress, which in turn may lead to raised blood pressure. On your own, use the body diagram to show how unforgiveness has affected you physically. (An example is shown below.) Ask the Holy Spirit to reveal this to you. Share your findings when you have completed this exercise in pairs. Persistent unforgiveness can cause us to become bitter and angry (Hebrews 12:15).

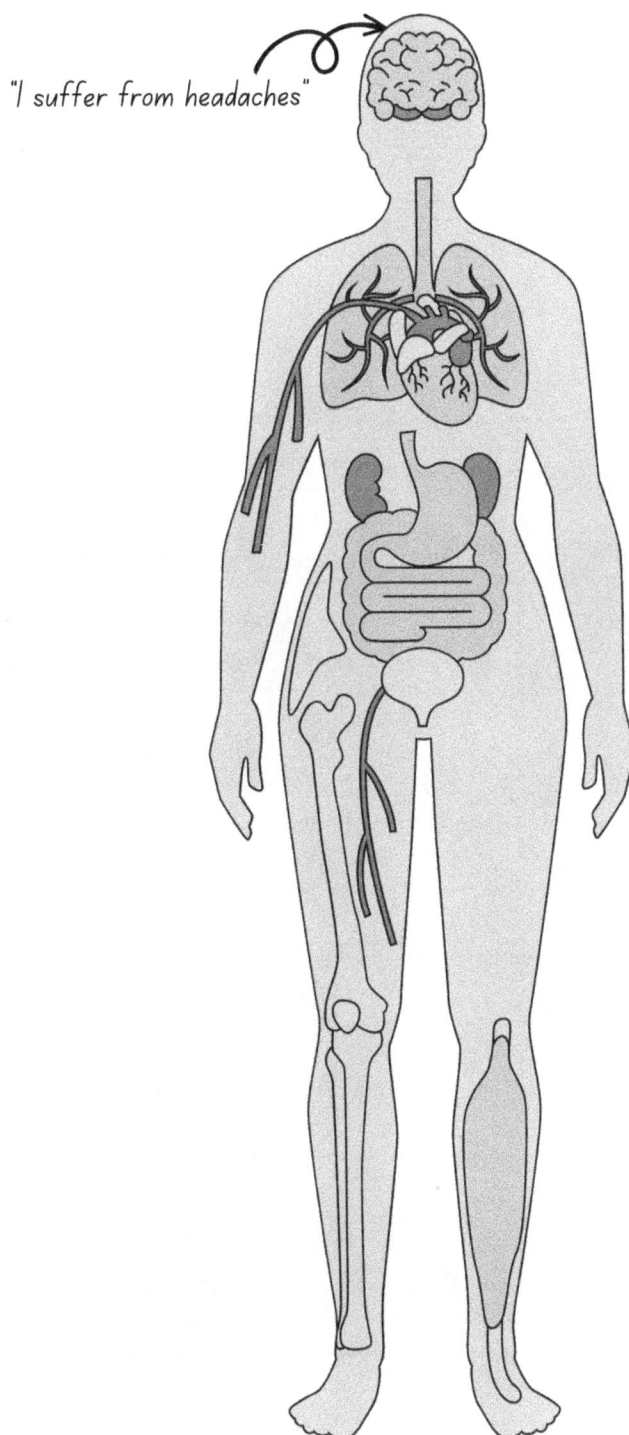

"I suffer from headaches"

what!

Exercise 4

Sometimes we need to forgive pronouncements or curses that were made over our lives; for example, 'My teacher, Mrs Sadd, said I would amount to nothing, and as a result, I never tried to achieve anything in life for fear of failure.'

- **Is this how you have responded?**
- List below the pronouncements or curses made over your life that you were aware of.

We must ask Christ to break these pronouncements/curses, but first we must repent and forgive our offenders.

1. ....
2. ....
3. ....
4. ....
5. ....
6. ....
7. ....
8. ....
9. ....
10. ....
11. ....
12. ....
13. ....
14. ....
15. ....

Please continue with a separate sheet if necessary.

Who do I need to forgive?

10 mins

Exercise 5

In pairs or threes, share **one** of your examples (sharing only what you can). Limit your time to 10 minutes each. Everyone should be able to share. If you work alone, share your insights with a trusted sister in Christ.

Remember to share:

1. How did you feel as a result of this injustice? What painful feelings did you experience?

2. How you changed your behaviour because of this injustice?

3. How you changed your behaviours towards others, yourself, and the situation?

4. How you feel about your environment, the world, your community, or your family?

5. What the injustice cost you in time, lost years, opportunities, etc?

6. **Keep to time. Share what you can in the larger group.**

Notes:

....

....

....

....

....

....

....

....

....

Resisting Forgiveness

10 mins

Exercise 6

How would you describe how easy it is for you to forgive? Avoid the temptation to respond to this question by saying, *"It depends on what/who it is."*

If you find it easy, well done! You should be able to witness the 'fruits' of the gift of forgiveness, i.e., the grace and mercy you extend to others. If the answer is **"no"**, spend time prayerfully reflecting on why this is. Ask the Holy Spirit to show you where you are resisting forgiving others. Share your findings with your sister(s) in Christ.

Reflections:

....

....

....

....

....

....

....

....

....

....

....

Let Me Let You into A Secret...

Matthew 6:14 (NKV)

"For if ye forgive men their trespasses, your heavenly Father will also forgive you."

Well, it's not really a secret!

Carrying unforgiveness in our hearts is a huge burden. We carry our 'unforgiveness burden' around with us everywhere we go. We sometimes pass down our unforgiving burdens to our families, our communities, and nations! Some people can discern the torment of a spirit of unforgiveness in us. This sinful behaviour seeps into every part of our lives. We try to contain it, but we just can't. The 'bitter fruits' of our unforgiveness toward others and ourselves are on view for all to see. The burden may be invisible to some, but it is NOT invisible to Christ. Christ can see ALL things.

What are the consequences of sin? Read the first part of Romans 6:23, "The wages of sin is death," but Christ atoned for our sin. He redeemed true believers from the curse of death and hell. Christ was the sacrificial Lamb of God who was slain to take away the sins of the world. Our sin was atoned for at the cross. When we accept Christ into our lives, confess Him as Lord and repent of our sins, we are forgiven as far as the East is from the West (Psalm 103:12). We are forgiven, **"and by His stripes, we are healed"** (Isaiah 53.5-KJV).

Carrying unforgiveness is a huge burden.

Imagine carrying this sack around with you every day. Many of us do!

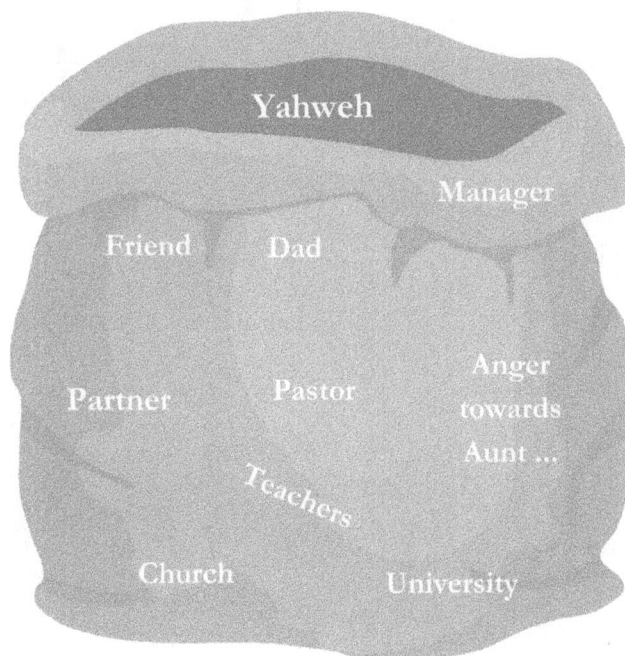

My Unjust Actions Towards Others...

Exercise 7

Sometimes, we are so caught up with what others have done to us that we forget that we, too, may be on someone's unforgiveness list. Remember the parable of the unmerciful servant (Matthew 18:21-35). Now it's time for you to list **YOUR** unjust actions towards others. Be specific with the incident. **For example, "When my friend did not answer my call, I did not answer her call, even though I knew she was going through a difficult time at work."**

Our unjust actions towards others may include ungodly behaviours towards countries, ethnic groups, and church brothers and sisters.

1. ....
2. ....
3. ....
4. ....
5. ....
6. ....
7. ....
8. ....
9. ....
10. ....
11. ....
12. ....
13. ....
14. ....
15. ....

Please continue with a separate sheet if necessary.

Unforgiveness: An Open Door to the Enemy

It would be irresponsible of me not to share with you the grave consequences of not letting go of the spirit of unforgiveness, both in the spiritual and in the natural.

Unforgiveness will give Satan and his army an open door to your life. It will prevent us from entering eternal rest with Christ.

Hebrews 12:15 warns us that unforgiveness is a sin that will cause bitterness in our lives. Bitterness can poison us and those around us, in a physical, mental, and spiritual sense. We must look to Genesis 4:1-8 to see how Cain's anger and bitterness led him to kill his brother out of jealousy towards him (a murdering spirit). Cain's murder of his brother opened the door to other spirits, such as a lying spirit; Cain lied, but the Lord revealed his sin.

For his punishment, Cain must leave his home. Cain is ashamed and responds in Genesis 4:13-14 (KJV):

> *‹13My punishment is greater than I can bear. 14Behold, thou hast driven me out this day from the face of the earth; and from thy face shall I be hid; and I shall be a fugitive and a vagabond in the earth; and it shall come to pass, that every one that findeth me shall slay me.›*

Cain's shame will not allow him to remain in his homeland (enter another unclean spirit – a spirit of shame). How ironic is that!

Cain's 'victim-like' response (a victim spirit) shows no remorse or repentance for what he has done. However, in His mercy, Yahweh offers Cain protection from being killed. In His mercy our Lord protects Cain with a 'mark'. Others will be hurt if they try to hurt or kill him. The Lord gives him safe passage.

Just from this short Bible story, we see how bitterness opened the door to other demonic spirits.

Ephesians 4:26-27 KJV warns us, **"26Be ye angry, and sin not: let not the sun go down upon your wrath: 27Neither give place to the devil."** Paul is saying that righteous anger is acceptable, but the ungodly expression of **anger is unacceptable** to Yahweh. It will lead you down a path of sin.

Let me remind you again that Christ commanded us to forgive, so that our Heavenly Father can forgive us (Matthew 6:14-15). This act of forgiveness has the power to transform our lives and bring us closer to our Heavenly Father.

Letting the sun go down on anger will only lead to feelings of bitterness, resentment, and unrighteous anger. We are warned not to let a bitter root spring up (Hebrews 12:15).

A Stronghold…

So, you might feel that you have repented and forgiven much, but you have yet to witness change and favour in your life. You may still feel stuck and keep experiencing painful situations in your life. If this is you, you may require deeper deliverance.

We have seen that once we open the door to the enemy (in our spirit, soul, and body), Satan and his army will seek to set up camp in our lives. They intend to be long-term tenants and will fight tooth and nail to avoid eviction. Satan's desire is not to see us free and wholly blameless before the Lord. Satan desires to "kill, steal and destroy" (John 10:10). Unforgiveness gives the enemy a free licence to do this.

Sometimes, the sin of unforgiveness is generational. Sometimes the sin of unforgiveness can be masked with other ungodly behaviours. The history books offer us evidence of nations, empires, clans, and families giving licence to the 'principal' spirit of unforgiveness for future generations.

For example, the transatlantic slave trade not only led to millions of murders, rape, and abuse of men, women, and children, but the residual impact has been phenomenal for past and current generations. The current generation still experiences generational trauma from the horrific pain their ancestors endured. Some of the demonic spirits attached to slavery are spirits of rejection, murder, abuse, deception, idolatry, witchcraft, poverty, paedophilia, fornication, and adultery, to name but a few. The enslavement of African peoples for over 400 years would mean that generations would suffer, even to this day. The struggle to repent and forgive those who have hurt us or our family enslaves many peoples and nations today. The Bible describes this as sin and can evoke generational curses on us, our families and nations, (Matthew 6:14-15 and Deuteronomy 5:9).

If you are a descendant of the effects of slavery (where your ancestors were slaves, slave traders, onlookers or even descendants of slaves and slave owners), I would strongly encourage you to seek the Lord in fasting, to repent of any agreements you may have made with these demonic spirits. Reject and rebuke these unclean spirits and seek freedom in Christ. Use the Holy Bible to guide you in your prayers but I also recommend some books of prayers and fasting to help you begin this process: **Ewing, Kevin L.A. (2023)** *Prayers That Work: Using Scriptures That Bring Change.* **Bahamas: Amazon Bookstore; and Mongomery, T. (2024)** *The Year of the Bride: Supernatural Strategy for Marital Breakthrough.* **Covered by God LLC.** *the Bride: Supernatural Strategy for Marital Breakthrough.* **Covered by God LLC.**

Our unforgiveness opens the door to the enemy, as we give him a foothold (Ephesians 4:27-29). Let us remind ourselves of what Yahweh tells us in Romans 12:19 (KJV), "vengeance is mine saith the Lord."

We must be willing to repent, forgive, and release into Yehovah's hands. He will repay us and our generation what is due. He is a 'just' judge! We have no right to adopt the position of judge over the lives of others. There is only one judge, and He sits on the throne in heaven.

Danger!

How do we keep our hearts clean from the sin of unforgiveness?

Unforgiveness can feel like layers of an onion. But Christ can bypass these layers, get straight to the core, and pull it out (I talk more about this on pages 176 and 178). Unforgiveness can be extremely difficult to overcome. It can be likened to a stubborn weed, which chokes all the good and fruitful seeds around it. Again, Christ can pull out and eradicate the stubborn weeds of unforgiveness in our lives, with our willing participation. Our role is to agree to this work on our hearts and to keep our hearts and minds clean from sin.

We will always be vulnerable to sin, because at the fall Adam and Eve (our ancestors) gave the devil a licence to reign on earth and, in turn, torment us. 1 Peter 5: 8 tells us to be watchful as Satan *"walketh about, seeking whom he may devour."* So, the devil is not seeking to have a coffee, a chat, or offer us support, but is seeking to "devour" us, "to kill, steal and destroy us" (John 10:10). Remember, Christ is victorious in overcoming the world (John 16:25-33).

The antidote to the sickness of unforgiveness (if not freely accepted) will result in eternal death and a relationship **without** the Godhead. So, we must not give the devil, his principalities, his powers, his rulers of the darkness of this world, a foothold in our lives (Ephesians 6:12 KJV).

Remember, our Heavenly Father will not forgive our trespasses unless we forgive others. Forgiveness is our release from prison.

Keeping Our 'House' Clean

The last thing I want to share is the importance of "keeping your house clean'. When Christ refers to a "house" in Matthew 12:43-45, he likens the house to us (the human spirit, soul, and body). So, for a fruitful and abundant relationship with our Heavenly Father, Son, and Holy Spirit, true repentance, forgiveness, prayer, and fasting are required. We need to keep our house in order.

The piece of scripture given on page 176 warns us of the dangerous consequences of poor prayer life, the absence of fasting, and an unrepentant, unforgiving heart.

"⁴³ When the unclean spirit is gone out of a man, he walketh through dry places, seeking rest, and findeth none. ⁴⁴Then he saith, I will return into my house from whence I came out; and when he is come, he findeth it empty, swept, and garnished. ⁴⁵Then goeth he, and taketh with himself seven other spirits more wicked than himself, and they enter in and dwell there: and the last state of that man is worse than the first. Even so shall it be also unto this wicked generation."

Matthew 12:43-45 KJV

What Does This Mean?

We **must** keep sin at bay; we must repent and forgive daily. We **must** be willing to come to Christ and pour out our hearts, pain, and disappointments. We **must** be willing to cast our cares onto Christ (1 Peter 5:7).

We **must** then be vigilant, keeping our 'house' and heart clean and purified to avoid deadlier spirits attaching themselves to our lives. Remember, these unclean spirits will **not** be squatters, because our unwillingness to forgive will give unclean spirits a free licence to move in and torment us in an even more. We have in effect given them a tenancy agreement.

The Stubborn Root...

If we are **not** seeing the blessings of Yehovah show up in our lives and the lives of our children (even when we have repented and forgiven those who have hurt us), we must follow the instructions given by Christ in Matthew 17:21. In Matthew 17:14-21, we see that Christ heals a demon-possessed boy. The disciples could not heal him. Why? Well, this demon was a superior level of demonic possession. Christ shows us that the 'stronghold' in this child's life **could not** be evicted unless the disciples prayed and fasted in faith. Deeper deliverance requires obedience, willingness, and commitment to be set free from oppressive spirits. We may need to break the demonic alters or covenants created and erected by ourselves or our ancestors knowingly or unknowingly.

Thinking Point?

I would also encourage you to reflect on how this child became demon possessed. Could it be due to his sin (possibly), or could it be generational? It's just something to consider.

Without 'deeper deliverance', we will not experience freedom in Christ. We will continue to feel stagnant. We will continue to experience failure and struggle with executing Yehovah's plans. We may still experience struggles with our health or experience poverty. This is all contrary to Yahweh's laws. Experiencing freedom will require regular prayer and fasting, led by the Holy Spirit. Otherwise, we will open wide the door to the enemy, who will bring seven more deadlier demons to take up residence in our lives.

Following the 'deeper deliverance' process, commands that we must keep a 'clean house'. Your Bible is your instruction manual for deliverance, but I recommend a life-changing book by Pastor Kevin L.A. Ewing. **The book is 'Prayers That Work: Using Scriptures That Bring Change'.** His teaching and video recordings have helped to deepen my understanding of Yahweh's laws and what He requires of His children. **Do not allow Satan free reign in your life.**

RECOVERY AND RECONCILIATION...

Sometimes, when we forgive others for hurting us, or indeed they forgive us, we desire reconciliation. Sometimes, this may not always be possible, especially if it is unsafe to do so. Our Father would never want to put His children in harm's way. However, let's look to the New Testament story of reconciliation with Christ.

Let's revisit Peter's denial of Christ before He was led to the cross to die for the atonement of our sins.

Luke 22:54-62 (KJV)

"⁵⁴ Then took they him, and led him, and brought him into the high priest's house. And Peter followed afar off.
⁵⁵ And when they had kindled a fire in the midst of the hall, and were set down together, Peter sat down among them. ⁵⁶ But a certain maid beheld him as he sat by the fire, and earnestly looked upon him, and said, This man was also with him.
⁵⁷ And he denied him, saying, Woman, I know him not.
⁵⁸ And after a little while another saw him, and said, Thou art also of them. And Peter said, Man, I am not.
⁵⁹ And about the space of one hour after another confidently affirmed, saying, Of a truth this fellow also was with him: for he is a Galilaean. ⁶⁰ And Peter said, Man, I know not what thou sayest. And immediately, while he yet spake, the cock crew.
⁶¹ And the Lord turned, and looked upon Peter. And Peter remembered the word of the Lord, how he had said unto him, Before the cock crow, thou shalt deny me thrice.
¹ And Peter went out and wept bitterly."

1. How might Peter have felt after the prophecy given by Christ was fulfilled? "You will deny me three times," (Luke 22:34).

2. Why do you think Christ asked Peter if he loved Him **three** times?

All is not lost. In John 21:15-19, we see a moving account of how Christ forgave Peter for denying Him three times. Christ not only forgave Peter but also reinstated him as an apostle in Christ. Peter died to self, so Christ could reign in him. When we genuinely repent, Christ restores us. Yahweh will restore the years the locusts have eaten (Joel 2:25-26).

Bringing It All Together...

- Forgiveness has to do with releasing our need to be judge and jury over another. We release the debt to Yahweh for His judgment. The Lord says vengeance is mine! (Deuteronomy 32:35). **What is Yahweh communicating here?**

- The act of forgiveness does not require us to have the offender(s) in our presence.

- Reconciliation will require true repentance and a sense of humility from the offender. It cannot be lip service.

- True forgiveness is the ultimate demonstration of our love for Christ and one another.

Maybe you feel that Yahweh will not serve out a just punishment to your offender. Scripture says, ***"For all have sinned and come short of the glory of God."*** Romans 3:23 KJV. You are in fact saying, "I don't trust Christ to sort this out, and I have never sinned."

Warning!

The Onion Effect

- Sometimes, forgiving others may be wrapped up in many 'layers' of pain. Many people or institutions may be involved in our pain, including our own actions or inactions.

- Unforgiveness may be steeped in history, and future generations may seek to hold onto unforgiveness for the sake of tradition.

- Sometimes, we feel that we have truly repented and forgiven those who have hurt us, and then we are faced with the individual/company/institution again and struggle to work with them or be in their company. We need to return to the Holy Spirit for revelation.

- Your desire to be a true believer and follow Christ's commands means we **must** reject long-held family or community beliefs against others. In such cases, ask yourself: **"Do I want to spend eternity with my King and Saviour, OR do I want to spend eternity in eternal jail?"** Only you have the power to choose.

- During such times, we must pray to the Holy Spirit for insight and guidance to reveal any blind spots and begin the process again.

Exercise 8

Have you really forgiven?

Below is a checklist to confirm whether you have truly forgiven those who have hurt you. Bring to mind situations where you experienced hurt at the hands of person, organisation institution etc, reflect on the following statements and tick all that apply:

- ☐ I get upset if the person(s) or institution or organisation's name is mentioned.
- ☐ I get anxious if the person(s) or institution or organisation makes contact with me.
- ☐ I lie awake thinking about how that person/organisation etc. has hurt me.
- ☐ I share my hurt with anyone who will listen.
- ☐ I have a rehearsed speech that I will recite to the offender(s) if I ever communicate with them in the future?
- ☐ I find any opportunity for me to punish individuals, organisations, institutions that have hurt me?
- ☐ I do my best to try and avoid this person/family, etc?
- ☐ I replay the same scenario repeatedly in my head, hoping for a different outcome?
- ☐ I imagine them confessing all to me and asking for fogiveness, hoping they will feel 10 times worse than what I have been feeling?
- ☐ I have regular reminders of how a person/institution offended me i.e. letters, photographs, e-mails etc.

If you have ticked any of the above, go to Christ in prayer to help heal and bind up your broken heart. Christ came to set the captives free.

Freedom & Release...

Truly repent. We must say what we mean. Yahweh will NOT be mocked (Galatian 6:7). Peter asked Christ, how many times must he forgive his brother. Christ responded, "..say not unto thee, Until seven times: but, Until seventy times seven," (Matthew 18:22 KJV).

This means we forgive endlessly as Christ forgives us.

If the pain we experience is too severe, speak to Christ, Our Comforter (2 Corinthians 1:3-4). The Holy Spirit may lead you to speak to a brother or sister in Christ, or a Christian Counsellor.

What will forgiveness give you?

☑ Freedom in Christ – Revisit the miracles of Christ in the New Testament.

☑ Reconciliation with Abba Father through His Son, Christ Yeshua.

☑ Reconciliation with the Holy Spirit of Yahweh

☑ Emotional stability.

☑ Emotional release, i.e. spiritual, mental, emotional, and physical healing.

☑ Release from tormented feelings and thoughts, or from feeling condemned.

☑ Freedom from being controlled by the past.

☑ Freedom from satanic attack.

☑ Freedom from emotional ties to those who have hurt you.

☑ Freedom from bitterness and hateful feelings.

☑ A closer walk with Christ Yeshua.

☑ Openness to Yahweh's plans for you going forward.

☑ A peace that surpasses all understanding.

☑ Openness to building and restoring relationships.

Can you think of any more life-changing benefits?

Reminder: Being led by the Holy Spirit:

☑ Repent of your unforgiving behaviour towards others and yourself.

☑ Ask Abba Father to forgive you for your unforgiving heart against others and yourself.

☑ If it is safe to do so, speak to the person/organisation/church and let them know you have been holding unforgiveness against them. (This is not an opportunity to throw stones but may be an opportunity to seek clarity). Remember, Satan will seek to confuse.

☑ Be willing to forgive and bless, whatever the outcome.

☑ Search your heart again and again to be sure you have forgiven those who have hurt you.

☑ Seek to make amends to restore trust. When we genuinely repent of our unforgiving nature, we should not carry on with hurtful behaviour towards self and others (Leviticus 6:5).

What have you learned about Yahweh's willingness to forgive those who truly repent?

Finally…

When we obey Yahweh's instruction and forgive those who have hurt us, Yahweh can release His blessings. Remember Abba Father reveals the following to His children, **"³ Blessed be the God and Father of our Lord Jesus Christ, who hath blessed us with all spiritual blessings in heavenly places in Christ: ⁴ According as he hath chosen us in him before the foundation of the world, that we should be holy and without blame before him in love,"** (Ephesians 1:3-4 KJV). Unforgiveness will cause delay and stagnation in our Christian Walk. We will not experience our full blessings stored up in heaven for us.

When we are willing to forgive, Abba Father promises us the following: **"²⁵ And I will restore to you the years that the locust hath eaten, the cankerworm, and the caterpiller, and the palmerworm, my great army which I sent among you. ²⁶ And ye shall eat in plenty, and be satisfied, and praise the name of the Lord your God, that hath dealt wondrously with you: and my people shall never be ashamed. ²⁷ And ye shall know that I am in the midst of Israel, and that I am the Lord your God, and none else: and my people shall never be ashamed,"** (Joel 2:25-27 KJV)

Decide to forgive today – it is not a choice, but a command Christ gave. It is time to walk in freedom today. Amen!

Call To Action

Dear Sister,

If you have managed to complete this chapter, well done. I can assure you that Christ is beginning His work in you and will see it through to its completion. Amen.

You may not be a believer in Christ, but you may have either come across the book by divine appointment and may be completing this workbook alone, or you may have been invited to join a Christian women's group to complete this workbook together. Maybe you are new to Christianity; whatever the reason, Christ Yeshua is calling you to be a member of His worldwide family. He wants to save you and redeem you from hell and eternity without Him. Maybe you are already a professed Christian, but your Christian Walk has gone cold or lukewarm. Remember what scripture says about the lukewarm Christian? Revelation 3:16 (KJV) says, *"I will spue thee out of my mouth."*

If this describes you, it is not too late to invite/reinvite Christ Yeshua into your heart and to commit to making Christ the Lord and Saviour of your life.

How might you do this?

Take your time and in a quiet space:

- Repent (express sincere regret or remorse about your sinful life).
- Ask Christ to forgive you and save you from the rightful penalty of eternal death (which you rightfully deserve).
- Confess with your mouth that Christ is Lord! Believe with your heart that Yahweh raised Christ Yeshua from the dead.
- If you willingly surrender and say this prayer, asking Christ Yeshua into your heart, spirit, soul, and mind, scripture says, 'You will be saved!'

Let me also share this amazing scripture with you, now that you have decided to follow Christ Yeshua. Luke 15:10 (KJV) says, *"Likewise, I say unto you, there is joy in the presence of the angels of God over one sinner that repenteth."*

Sister in Christ, Heaven is rejoicing!

Homework 7

Task 1

Spend time with Christ Yeshua in prayer and conversation.

- Share your feelings with Christ about the pain of unforgiveness in your life and its effect on you.
- Share your feelings with Christ about the pain of not being forgiven by someone you love or care about.
- Write a journal laying bare your pain.
- Be prepared to share what you can in next week's lesson or with a sister in Christ.

Next Week's Session

If working as a group: Facilitators should seek the permission of the group to add **thirty minutes** to your next session for the sharing of testimonies. If working alone, consider the possibility of sharing your testimony with your church.

Task 2

Next Week's Task:

Working in a group – All group members must:

- Prepare a five-minute testimony (you will be timed) of what Christ has done in your life over the past seven weeks.
- You can deliver or present your testimony, i.e. a poem, a song, a creative writing piece, singing, painting, any creative artwork.
- Testimonies will take place at the end of the final taught session.
- The group must keep strict time boundaries. **It is important that everyone has an opportunity to share their testimony.**
- If completing this programme alone, share your testimony with your church brothers and sisters.

END OF MODULE 7

Homework:

Homework:

187

MODULE 8
WALK IN YOUR CALLING

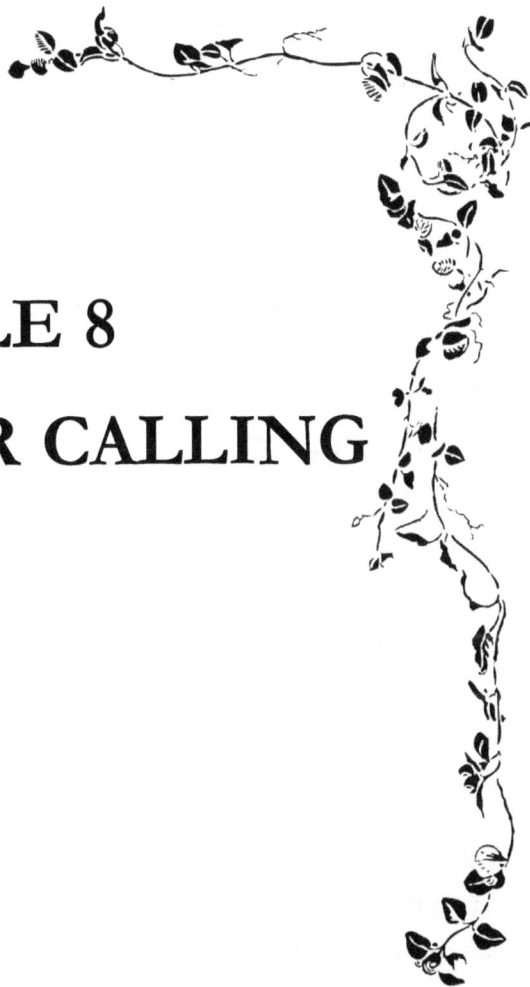

Chapter 8: Walk In Your Calling

"¹⁵ And unto one he gave five talents, to another two,
and to another one; to every man according
to his several ability; and straightway took his journey."
Matthew 25`;15 (KJV)

Opening Prayer:

Group Contract:

If you are completing this programme within a group, I would strongly advise that you remind participants of the importance of adhering to and remaining committed to the group contract. Revisit the contract at the start of each session to ensure the safety of the group. It is important that the group adhere to it.

Module Eight – Reflection

If working as a group, set aside 15 minutes to share your personal reflections from Module 7. **Please keep to time boundaries.**

Session Reflections

Over the past seven weeks, we have been on a personal and/or collective journey with the Godhead. We began with 'Intimacy with Christ Yeshua', then explored our worth, how we see ourselves, and how Christ sees us. We have explored emotive issues such as:

- Our self-worth and self-esteem.
- The pain of rejection.
- Our struggles with fear.
- Our struggles with anger.
- The masks we wear to hide our pain.
- Repentance and forgiveness; and finally in Module 8 we will explore,
- Walking in your Calling/Gifts and talents.

The module will end with a message of encouragement that Christ wants you to hear. Remember what Christ told us in John 16:33? Christ has overcome all our pain, rejection, sadness, pain, and anger, etc. Christ overcame all this in His death on the cross, His resurrection and ascension into heaven (John 19:30).

Session 8: In this module, we will be exploring - 'Walk in Your Calling'.

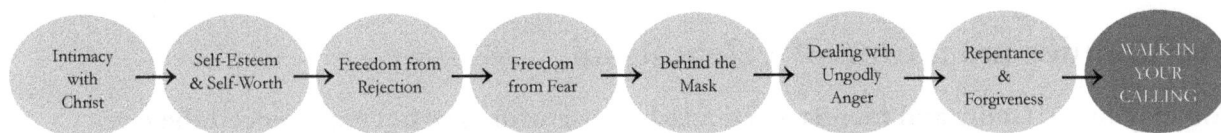

Intimacy with Christ → Self-Esteem & Self-Worth → Freedom from Rejection → Freedom from Fear → Behind the Mask → Dealing with Ungodly Anger → Repentance & Forgiveness → WALK IN YOUR CALLING

Session Aims

So, in our final session, you will be:

- Reviewing your learning and understanding about the spiritual gifts of Yahweh that He has blessed us with through His spirit, and why we are instructed to use our gifts.
- Explore our God-given gifts and talents and how to use them by continually walking and listening to the Holy Spirit.
- Explore why you may have yet to use and share your heavenly gifts.
- Sharing your testimony with others.

Remember in Module One (Page 4), where you explored the parable of the Vinedresser (Matthew 21:33-46)? The parable informs the believer that the vinedresser will cut off unfruitful branches and throw them into the fire if they are not bearing fruit.

Session Outcomes

By the end of the session, delegates will be able to:
- Identify the gifts and talents that Yahweh has gifted us with.
- Identify the ways we are actively using these gifts and talents.

Time for Testimonies

Working in a group

Whilst there will not be a formal check-in for this session (if you are in a group), you must reserve time to share your testimony. To ensure everyone has a chance to speak, please keep your testimonies to a maximum of three minutes each if you're in a group of five or more.

Testimonies are a time of celebration!

You may invite family and friends, particularly those who have not experienced the love of Christ in their lives. However, they may have witnessed your transformation whilst studying on this programme; including your deepening relationship with Christ and your love of God's word. If you decide to share your testimonies with friends and family, leave testimonies until the end of the session.

I strongly encourage you to share the good news of Christ's healing in your life, as sharing our testimony increases our faith (Revelation 12:11).

Exercise 1

1. Prayerfully explore the ways in which you are being obedient or disobedient to the will of Yehovah when you use/do not use your talents for the work of the Kingdom.

2. Share your personal testimony of how the Lord has worked in your life throughout this programme.

Dear Sister in Christ,

Welcome to your final workbook in the
'Healing Eve' – Inner Healing Programme
Daughters in Christ.

Congratulations!
Number eight in the Bible is associated with new
beginnings, and now that you have reached the final
module, I do not doubt that the Holy Spirit has
done some mighty work in you over the past
few weeks or months.
My prayer for you is that the Holy Spirit has
guided you to surrender your pain and
disappointments to Christ, so that you can
move away from the pain that lies in your heart.
Remember what it says in
Philippians 1:6 (KJV):

"Being confident of this very thing,
that he which hath begun a good work in you will
perform it until the day of Jesus Christ."
It is important for you to know that you were
bought/purchased for a high price from the
prince of this world (Satan). Christ paid your
ransom with His precious blood.
Yahweh sacrificed His only begotten Son for You!

Scripture Reading

Matthew 25:14-30 (KJV)

The Parable of the Talents

"¹⁴ For the kingdom of heaven is as a man travelling into a far country, who called his own servants, and delivered unto them his goods.

¹⁵ And unto one he gave five talents, to another two, and to another one; to every man according to his several ability; and straightway took his journey.

¹⁶ Then he that had received the five talents went and traded with the same, and made them other five talents. ¹⁷ And likewise he that had received two, he also gained other two.

¹⁸ But he that had received one went and digged in the earth, and hid his lord's money.

¹⁹ After a long time the lord of those servants cometh, and reckoneth with them.

²⁰ And so he that had received five talents came and brought other five talents, saying, Lord, thou deliveredst unto me five talents: behold, I have gained beside them five talents more.

²¹ His lord said unto him, Well done, thou good and faithful servant: thou hast been faithful over a few things, I will make thee ruler over many things: enter thou into the joy of thy lord.

²² He also that had received two talents came and said, Lord, thou deliveredst unto me two talents: behold, I have gained two other talents beside them.

²³ His lord said unto him, Well done, good and faithful servant; thou hast been faithful over a few things, I will make thee ruler over many things: enter thou into the joy of thy lord.

²⁴ Then he which had received the one talent came and said, Lord, I knew thee that thou art an hard man, reaping where thou hast not sown, and gathering where thou hast not strawed:

²⁵ And I was afraid, and went and hid thy talent in the earth: lo, there thou hast that is thine.

²⁶ His lord answered and said unto him, Thou wicked and slothful servant, thou knewest that I reap where I sowed not, and gather where I have not strawed:

²⁷ Thou oughtest therefore to have put my money to the exchangers, and then at my coming I should have received mine own with usury.

²⁸ Take therefore the talent from him, and give it unto him which hath ten talents.

²⁹ For unto every one that hath shall be given, and he shall have abundance: but from him that hath not shall be taken away even that which he hath.

³⁰ And cast ye the unprofitable servant into outer darkness: there shall be weeping and gnashing of teeth."

Scripture Reflections

Matthew 25:14-30 KJV

Exercise 2

Class Discussion... (15 mins)

On your own (five mins), take a moment to prayerfully reflect on:

1. How did this piece of scripture speak to you about the gifts and talents Yahweh has blessed you with?

2. Make a list of the talents that you believe the Lord has blessed you with.

3. Share your reflections with your group or with a trusted sister in Christ.

Reflections:

_____

_____

_____

_____

_____

_____

_____

_____

_____

_____

_____

_____

_____

_____

Spiritual Gifts...

Exercise 3

In groups, explore what you understand by the term:

Spiritual Gifts _____

_____

_____

_____

_____

Definition...

Spiritual gifts are what every believer is given when they receive the gift of Salvation. Just as the gift of Salvation by grace through faith, our spiritual gifts **cannot** operate without our faith in Yahweh. Abba Father is so generous; He is constantly giving us gifts.

He gave the world His only begotten son, Christ Yeshua; the greatest gift of all to all humanity. Christ had all the gifts of the Holy Spirit to share with others whilst on earth. Our Creator generously divides out His gifts to us..

You may ask, **"How does Yahweh's spirit work in us?"** Let us look at the Greek word **'Pneumatikos'.** The word 'pneumatikos' relates to our human spirit, or the rational part of ourselves linked with our soul. Our soul is our will and emotions. Our soul will agree or disagree with Yahweh's plan for us to be His instrument.

When we are filled with and governed by the Holy Spirit of Yahweh, we have His strength in us to do all the things that Yahweh requires of us. When Christ began his mission on earth (Matthew 3:16-17), he knew that being filled with the Holy Spirit meant that Christ could do all His Father sent Him to do on earth. Christ healed the sick; He gave sight to the blind; He fed the poor; He forgave sins. We too can **"do all things in Christ who strengthens us"** Philippians 4:13. The Spirit of Yahweh is now in us, and we are now alive in Christ!

The beautiful thing was that when Christ received the Holy Spirit, He had the power to share it with His disciples, who performed miracles just like Him. Christ then promised us that if we believe in Him and the works that He did on earth, then we too shall perform miracles and even greater works than He (John 14:12).

Now let's look at the word *'Charismata'*. Charismata is the ability to be inspired by the Holy Spirit (reflecting our Lord Christ Yeshua). Being inspired by Christ enables us to enter a realm that we are incapable of entering ourselves, solely for us to enrich the body of Christ and fulfil our purpose in Him.

The source of a spiritual gift never lies in the person who possesses it but in the person who gives it. Our spiritual gifts must bring glory to Yahweh.

Reflections:

_____

_____

_____

_____

_____

_____

_____

_____

_____

_____

_____

_____

_____

Scripture Reading...

It is essential to understand the context in which Yahweh shares His gifts with us (His children). In our human form, we may feel we have inherited specific gifts from our ancestors; for example, we may be blessed with the gift of singing, dancing, and writing, which are all blessings, but are all 'gifts' given from Yahweh. The Word of God is very specific.

Read the scripture out loud together in the group or alone.

1 Corinthians 12:3-11 (KJV)

"*³ Wherefore I give you to understand, that no man speaking by the Spirit of God calleth Jesus accursed: and that no man can say that Jesus is the Lord, but by the Holy Ghost.*

⁴ Now there are diversities of gifts, but the same Spirit.

⁵ And there are differences of administrations, but the same Lord.

⁶ And there are diversities of operations, but it is the same God which worketh all in all.

⁷ But the manifestation of the Spirit is given to every man to profit withal.

⁸ For to one is given by the Spirit the word of wisdom; to another the word of knowledge by the same Spirit;

⁹ To another faith by the same Spirit; to another the gifts of healing by the same Spirit;

¹⁰ To another the working of miracles; to another prophecy; to another discerning of spirits; to another divers kinds of tongues; to another the interpretation of tongues:

¹¹ But all these worketh that one and the selfsame Spirit, dividing to every man severally as he will."

Exercise 4

Reflect on this piece of scripture and the nine gifts the Holy Spirit gives. Which of these nine gifts do you sense the Holy Spirit has blessed you with? Write them below:

1. _____

2. _____

3. _____   (10mins)

In pairs or on your own, prayerfully reflect on whether you are: (10mins)

- Walking and utilising these gifts as the Lord leads you, or are your gifts hidden in the attic or basement of your heart and mind?

- Are there any spiritual gifts that you want to be blessed with, and why?

Important!

We cannot in any way compare our Heavenly Father with that of our earthly parents. We may feel we have grown up in a family where Yahweh's gifts were discouraged.

Gifts can be physical, like a birthday present or a kind act, but gifts can also be words of kindness or encouragement. **Did you experience these types of gifts growing up? What if you were always made to feel small and insignificant because it appeared as if you were not gifted? In such cases, we may believe that:**

- Yahweh loves us less. For example, you may say, **"Lord, you must love my sister more because you have given her four gifts, and I only have been blessed with one."** It is essential to realise that heavenly gifts relate to your purpose (our calling). We are all called for a specific purpose: to advance and proclaim the Kingdom of Yahweh, and we all have a unique part to play in Yahweh's Kingdom. Therefore, not all gifts may be required. **Read Ephesians 1:3.**
- Our gift(s) are only relevant to the Body of Christ to glorify Yahweh **not** ourselves.

It is important that we avoid this way of thinking.

The Holy Spirit, throughout history, has gifted particular people for specific tasks in both the Old and New Testaments. For example:

- Moses – prophecy, teaching, exhorting, service, leading, giving – Exodus, Leviticus, Numbers, and Deuteronomy
- Bezalel – artistic work for the Temple – Exodus 31:2-5
- Joshua – Spirit of Wisdom – Exodus 33, Deuteronomy 34:9
- John the Baptist – Evangelist – Luke 1:30
- Mary – Servitude – Luke 1:35
- David – Psalmist/Worship – Samuel 23:2
- Christ Yeshua on earth – **(all spiritual gifts)** Matthew, Mark, Luke, and John.

Remember that Christ possessed all gifts of the Holy Spirit.

When we submit to Christ, we are open to being directed by the Holy Spirit. We should then witness change in our lives. We will also witness the development of new fruits to assist us in our calling. Revisit the gospels to see how Christ used His gifts to glorify His Father in heaven.

Exercise 5 (five mins – pairs)

Q. How evident are the fruits of the Holy Spirit in your life?

1. Spiritual gifts are given so we can worship and serve our Lord. These gifts are used to build up His church and His heavenly kingdom – 1 Corinthians 12:71. **Can you think of any other scriptures demonstrating this?**

2. Every Christian disciple has spiritual gifts. Yahweh uses these gifts to accomplish His purpose – 1 Peter 4:10.

3. Some of us reject these gifts, or we feel we do not deserve them. Such an undeserving response can be rooted in our early childhood experiences, heavy shepherding or rebellion. It may also be rooted in listening to the enemy's voice instead of Yahweh's voice. If this is you, read Luke 11:13. **What is the Apostle Luke trying to communicate to Yahweh's children?**

4. Scripture also tells us to **"Ask, and it shall be given you; seek, and ye shall find; knock, and it shall be opened unto you."** Matthew 7:7 (KJV) – **What gifts do you want to ask Yahweh for today?**

Exercise 6

Working alone or in pairs, and (without looking at the next page) jot down some notes under each heading below as to what these gifts mean for you as a daughter in Christ.

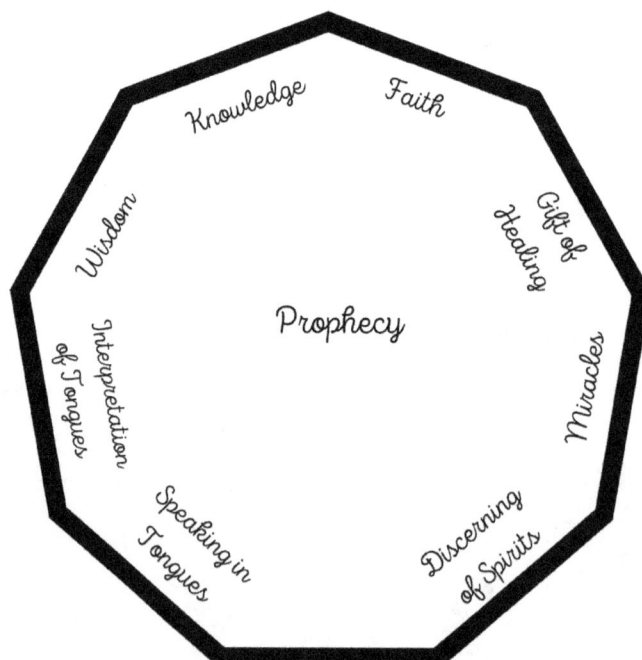

Knowledge   Faith

Wisdom

Gift of Healing

Interpretation of Tongues

Prophecy

Miracles

Speaking in Tongues

Discerning of Spirits

The Meaning of Numbers: The Number 9

The number '9' is used 49 times in Scripture. The number 9 is associated with divine completeness or conveys the meaning of finality. In John 19:30, Christ cried out, "It is finished." Christ died at hour nine of the day to make the way of Salvation open to everyone. Christ's mission was completed, and He left us His gifts to build His church and to glorify Yehovah.

These are the Nine gifts of the Holy Spirit; let's have a look at them now...

1. **Wisdom** – the divine ability to speak a word that is right for the situation and is given by Yahweh – **1 Kings 3:16-28.**

2. **Knowledge** – the divine ability to know something only Yahweh knows, and to share this knowledge with others. We see this demonstrated by Yahweh's prophets – **1 Corinthians 2:3.**

3. **Faith** – the ability to believe Yahweh for things others have little or no faith in – **Hebrews 11:1.**

4. **Healing** – the divine ability to heal sickness and disease in the name of Christ Yeshua. – **Acts 3:1-10.**

5. **Miracles** – the divine ability to perform mighty acts of God – **Exodus, Acts 19:11**.

6. **Discerning spirits** – the divine ability to distinguish between human spirit, demonic spirit, and the Spirit of God – **Acts 16:16–18.**

7. **Prophecy** – the divine ability to receive and communicate an immediate message from God what will happen in the future – **Acts 11:27-28.**

8. **Tongues** – the divine ability to speak to Yahweh in a language never learned. Comes out of the person's human spirit and not the person's mind – **1 Corinthians 14:13–19; Mark 16:17.**

9. **Interpretation of tongues** – the divine ability to interpret what individual tongues mean – **1 Corinthians 14:26–28.**

IMPORTANT

☑ We must be thankful for our heavenly gifts – **Matthew 16:8-10.**

☑ Spiritual gifts must be exercised and tested in an orderly to give glory to God. Remember, in the book of Exodus, the Pharaoh's sorcerers could replicate a few (not all) of the miracles initially performed by Yahweh through his servant, Moses (These gifts were not from Yahweh) – **1 Corinthians 14:23–32.**

☑ The outworking of our heavenly gifts should be done in love – **1 Corinthians 13:1.**

Exercise 8

Which of the above gifts has Yahweh blessed you with?

1. _____
2. _____
3. _____
4. _____
5. _____
6. _____

Which additional gifts would you like Yahweh to bless you with, and why?

1._____

2._____

3._____

4._____

5._____

6._____

7._____

Personal Reflection Points:

Reflect on the gifts you have and how you have been using them?

Exercise 9

How Much Are You Using Your Spiritual Gifts?

OVERFLOWING

To what degree do you use your gifts from Yahweh? (draw a line) You may want to draw separate lines for each spiritual gift you have been blessed with.

UNDER UTILISED

Q. Indicate on the beaker, how much you are exercising your spiritual gifts. Are you 'overflowing', or are your gifts being underutilised? Please discuss your reasons with your group or a trusted sister in Christ.

It is important to remember that:

- Sometimes parents, family churches, brothers and sisters in Christ, etc., do not encourage us to use our heavenly gifts, but remember what Christ said in John 14:12: **In a nutshell, this passage informs us that the gifts of Yahweh are not for yesterday; they are for today, and Christ will continue to work through us if we let Him. Not using our gifts is an act of disobedience.**

- **Reminder! Our gifts are not for our use; they are to glorify Yahweh and bless others.**

- When we are obedient and use our heavenly gifts as instructed, these gifts will be a blessing to others. Do you remember the woman at the well? (John 4) Christ prophesied about her sinful life, and she was stunned, so much so that she went and testified of Christ to others, and they believed. Others believed, even though they were not present during this encounter. Another of her blessings was the gift of evangelism.

How have you used your heavenly gift(s) to share the good news of Christ with unbelievers?

Romans 12: Motivational and Spiritual Gifting in the Church...

Now that we have learnt about the gifts of the Holy Spirit, we can briefly look at various spiritual roles Yahweh has created to exercise some or all these gifts. I would like to add that we can exercise our God-given gifts without a specific position. We should exercise these as human beings, parents, siblings, etc. Having a title/role does not give us status amongst others. Still, a title/role demands more of us concerning accountability and responsibility (Luke 12:48).

Let us briefly look at some of these roles:

Evangelist – a special ability to share the gospel and bring others to faith in Christ – Ephesians 4:11-14; Acts 21:8, 8:5-6; 26-40,14:21.

Pastor – a special ability to shepherd Christ's church – Ephesians 4:11–14; 1 Timothy 3:1-7. Be reminded that the pastor may not be good in all these gifts.

Apostle – a special ability to plant Christian churches and to establish local leadership – Ephesians 4:11; 1 Corinthians 15:5,7; Romans 1:1,11:13.

Teacher – a special ability to instruct, communicate, and enable others to understand and receive God's truth through His word – Ephesians 4:11 –14; Corinthians 12:28.

Prophet – a special ability to receive and communicate the heart of God – Ephesians 4:11–14; 1Corinthians 12:10.

Service (ministry) – a special ability to identify care for others willingly and to make use of Yahweh's resources - Romans 12:7 and 2 Timothy 1: 16–18

Exhortation – a special ability to comfort, strengthen, counsel and encourage – Romans 12:8; Hebrews 10:25

Giving – a special ability to support others, whether it be financial, by support, offering a listening ear, etc. – Romans 12:8.

Leadership (Administration) – a special ability to advance Yahweh's will and purpose for His bride. God-appointed leaders is scriptural – Romans 12:8.

Mercy – a special ability to feel genuine empathy and compassion for the distressed and to translate it into practical help – Romans 12:8; Luke 10:33-34.

Hospitality – a special ability to make others feel welcome and provide food and accommodation to those in need – Romans 12:3; 1; Timothy 3:2; 1 Peter 4:9.

Celibacy (self-control) – special ability to remain single as a calling in life — 1 Corinthians 7:7-8; Matthew 19:10-12.

Exercise 10

Now that you have had the opportunity to study all Yahweh's gifts and the roles of Yahweh's Kingdom, honestly reflect on:

1. **How well are you using your motivational gifts of the Spirit?**
2. **How well are you executing your God-given role(s)?**
3. **What new gifts or heaven-ordained roles would you prayerfully like to request from Abba Father?**
4. **Which heavenly roles are you resisting, and why?**

It is essential that your requests are Spirit-led and are not based on what sister 'So&So' at Church is blessed with. We are all unique, and Abba Father requires us to use His gifts in a particular way, with specific people/animals/His creation, in a certain part of His Kingdom. So, His part of the world may be your street, community, or workplace or, like the Apostles, worldwide.

Different gifts and roles are given according to the grace given to us by our faith in Christ Yeshua.

Ask yourself: How much faith do I have in Christ?

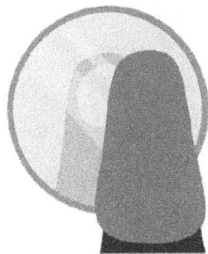

Please feel free to take time out for some prayerful reflection.
Earnestly listen to what the Holy Spirit is laying on your heart.
Then, in pairs/three, share with your sisters in Christ what the Lord has spoken.

Ask your Sisters in Christ to pray for you and with you to fully walk in your calling and for more of His beautiful gifts in your life.

Do You Remember Module 1?

I just wanted to remind you...

- **What did the scripture tell us about the danger of not bearing fruit?**
- **What will the Vinedresser do (Yahweh) if we do not use our Spiritual gifts?**

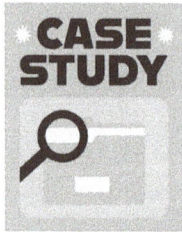

CASE STUDY

Exercise 11

Now let's look at the case study of Belinda and Beverley. Read this through together in your group or alone.

The Case of Belinda & Beverley

Belinda and Beverley were born into the same family, having access to the same parents and, as much as possible, having the same opportunities. They had different talents and abilities, and up until they were 16, they were both content and happy.

Belinda and Beverley took very different paths in life. Belinda chose to continue her studies, get a job, meet her husband, settle in the suburbs, and have children. Belinda experienced everyday life's normal ups and downs but attended church every Sunday and helped by serving coffee every Sunday after church service. Belinda was well-liked and a very supportive church member; Belinda was held in very high regard by her church brothers and sisters.

Beverley, however, found it difficult to settle into college life and struggled to attend church. Beverley decided to find a job in the city and was known to work and play hard. Unfortunately, Beverley became involved with the wrong crowd and began taking drugs to maintain her work performance. Beverley slowly became an addict, and after a two-year addiction, losing her job, and being estranged from her family, Beverley volunteered to go to rehab. After two years in and out of rehab, Beverley began to return to church; she eventually gave her life to Christ.

Beverley then created a programme for those suffering from drug addiction or in recovery. Her church supported her and eventually helped her develop and expand to launch her own charity. Given her history of drug taking, Beverley was unable to have children but was seen as one of the 'mothers' of the church, providing prayer, support, a listening ear, and guidance to all troubled children she met inside and outside of the church.

Q. Discussion Point: (10 minutes)

1. How were both sisters demonstrating/utilising their God-given gifts?
2. Prayerfully, ask the Holy Spirit which of the sisters' lives resonates with you, and why.

Walking with Christ Yeshua will ensure that the fruits and gifts of the Holy Spirit will develop in our lives. When we are born again, the Ruach of Yahweh dwells within us and makes us a part of His worldwide church – Ephesians 2:21.

As members of His church, we need to remain active in our gifts; even if we cannot walk or talk, we can still praise, pray, and worship the King of Kings and the Lord of Lords.

The Holy Spirit will:

- Reveal the secret things of Yahweh if we remain in the Vine that is Christ Yeshua – Ephesians 1:17.
- The Holy Spirit will place his seal over us to guarantee our inheritance in His heavenly Kingdom – Ephesians 1:13-14.
- The Holy Spirit will empower us to be a witness of Christ wherever we are – Acts 1:8.

Read the transformation of the Apostle Peter and Paul. They allowed the Holy Spirit to guide them so they may be a blessing to **all** nations by spreading the good news of Christ Yeshua.

As we humble ourselves before the Godhead, we will experience
progressive change and transformation. The Lord will see
His work through to its completion, (Philippians 1:6).

"I am the true vine, and my
Father is the husbandman.

² Every branch in me that beareth not
fruit he taketh away: and every branch
that beareth fruit, he purgeth it,
that it may bring forth more fruit."

John 15:1-2 (KJV)

Daughters of the King, it is essential that we testify to the healing transformation that has taken place in our lives after completing these modules. Some of you may not have witnessed any change or transformation, but please do not give up hope. Keep fasting, praying, and studying the Word of God. The Ruach of Yahweh is moving, and the Lord promises us in Philippians 1:6 (KJV), *"Being confident of this very thing, that he which hath begun a good work in you will perform it until the day of Jesus Christ."* Amen.

! Be reminded as we walk in our calling

Revelation 12:10-12 (NKJV)

"10 And I heard a loud voice saying in heaven, Now is come salvation, and strength, and the kingdom of our God, and the power of his Christ: for the accuser of our brethren is cast down, which accused them before our God day and night.

11 And they overcame him by the blood of the Lamb, and by the word of their testimony; and they loved not their lives unto the death.

12 Therefore rejoice, ye heavens, and ye that dwell in them. Woe to the inhabiters of the earth and of the sea! for the devil is come down unto you, having great wrath, because he knoweth that he hath but a short time."

Final Note from the Author

I pray that this workbook has blessed you profoundly. The Holy Spirit is indescribable and unfathomable! I was blessed to be in the presence of the Godhead as I typed, prayed, reflected, and studied His Word. The Bible tells us that Yahweh's laws are written in our hearts; His laws are our food, sustenance, and protection.

My earnest prayer for you is that this workbook will be a catalyst for your growth in faith in Christ Yeshua and His divine plans for you and your ministry.

God Bless, Sister in Christ

Call To Action

Dear Sister,

If you have completed this book, well done! I can assure you that Christ is beginning His work in you and will see it through to its completion. Amen.

You may not be a believer in Christ, but you may have either come across the book by divine appointment and may be completing this workbook alone, or you may have been invited to join a Christian women's group to complete this workbook together. Maybe you are new to Christianity; whatever the reason, Christ Yeshua is calling you to be a member of His worldwide family. He wants to save you and redeem you from hell and eternity without Him.

Maybe you are already a professed Christian, but your Christian Walk has gone cold or lukewarm. Remember what scripture says about the lukewarm Christian? Revelation 3:16 (KJV) says, ***"I will spue thee out of my mouth."***

If this describes you, it is not too late to invite/reinvite Christ Yeshua into your heart and to commit to making Christ the Lord and Saviour of your life.

How might you do this?

Take your time and in a quiet space:

- Repent (express sincere regret or remorse about your sinful life).
- Ask Christ to forgive you and save you from the rightful penalty of eternal death (which you rightfully deserve).
- Confess with your mouth that Christ is Lord! Believe with your heart that Yahweh raised Christ Yeshua from the dead.
- If you willingly surrender and say this prayer, asking Christ Yeshua into your heart, spirit, soul, and mind, scripture says, 'You will be saved!'

Let me also share this amazing scripture with you, now that you have decided to follow Christ Yeshua. Luke 15:10 (KJV) says, *"Likewise, I say unto you, there is joy in the presence of the angels of God over one sinner that repenteth."*

Sister in Christ, Heaven is rejoicing!

Homework 8

- Pray and seek Yahweh's guidance on how you have honoured the gifts Abba Father has given you.
- Creative work: Make time to be alone with Abba Father. Ask the Holy Spirit to reveal any blocks you may have that are preventing you from walking in your calling.
- Truly repent and seek forgiveness for neglecting or being disobedient in not using your spiritual gifts as the Holy Spirit has asked you to.
- Walk in your forgiveness (Psalm 103:12).
- Pray and seek the Lord's guidance on your next steps (Psalm 37:5).
- Complete your Module 8 journal, reflecting on your own spiritual gifting.
- Share your reflections with a sister in Christ in your fellowship.

THE END

Extra Templates

Reflections

Reflections

Reflections

Reflections

Template 2: 'Roots & Fruits' Tree – Anger

Template 3: The 'Anger' Iceberg

What's Lies Beneath The ANGER?

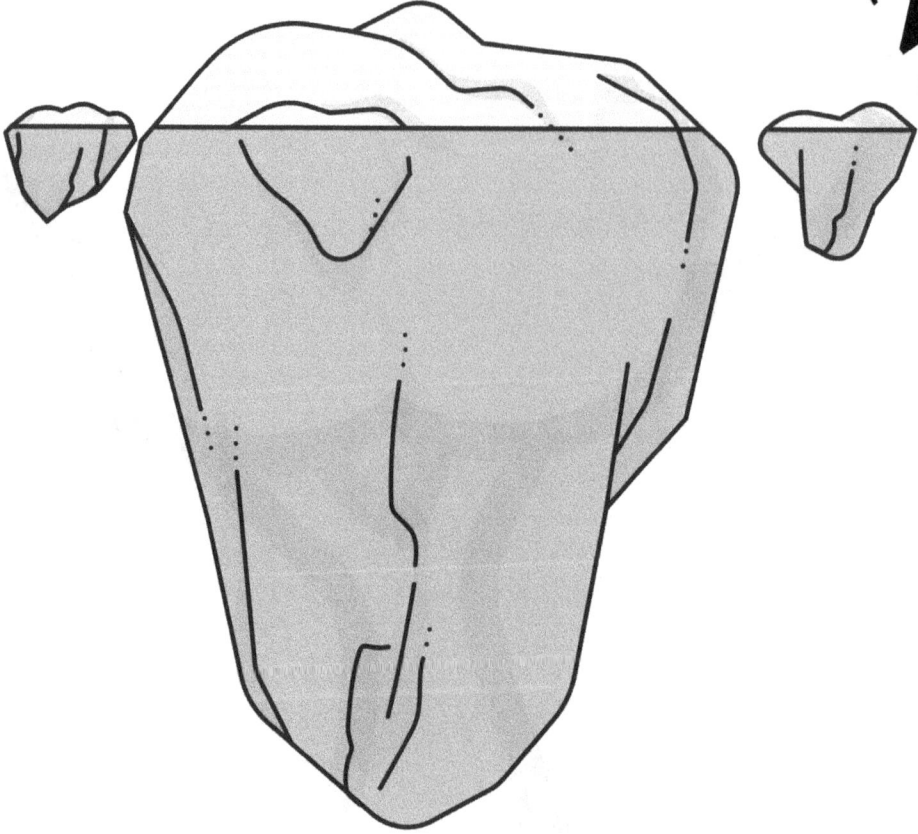

Template 4 – Anger List

Prayerfully ask the Holy Spirit to show you who you are still angry with and write them out in the boxes below.

No.	Family/Loved ones	Friends/Church Family	Colleagues	Organisations (school, employers, hospitals, etc.)
1.				
2.				
3.				
4.				
5.				
6.				
7.				
8.				
9.				
10.				
11.				
12.				
13.				
14.				
15.				
16.				
17.				
18.				
19.				
20.				
21.				
22.				
23.				
24.				

Template 5: 'Roots & Fruits' Tree of Fear

Template 6: What 'Masks' Do I Wear?

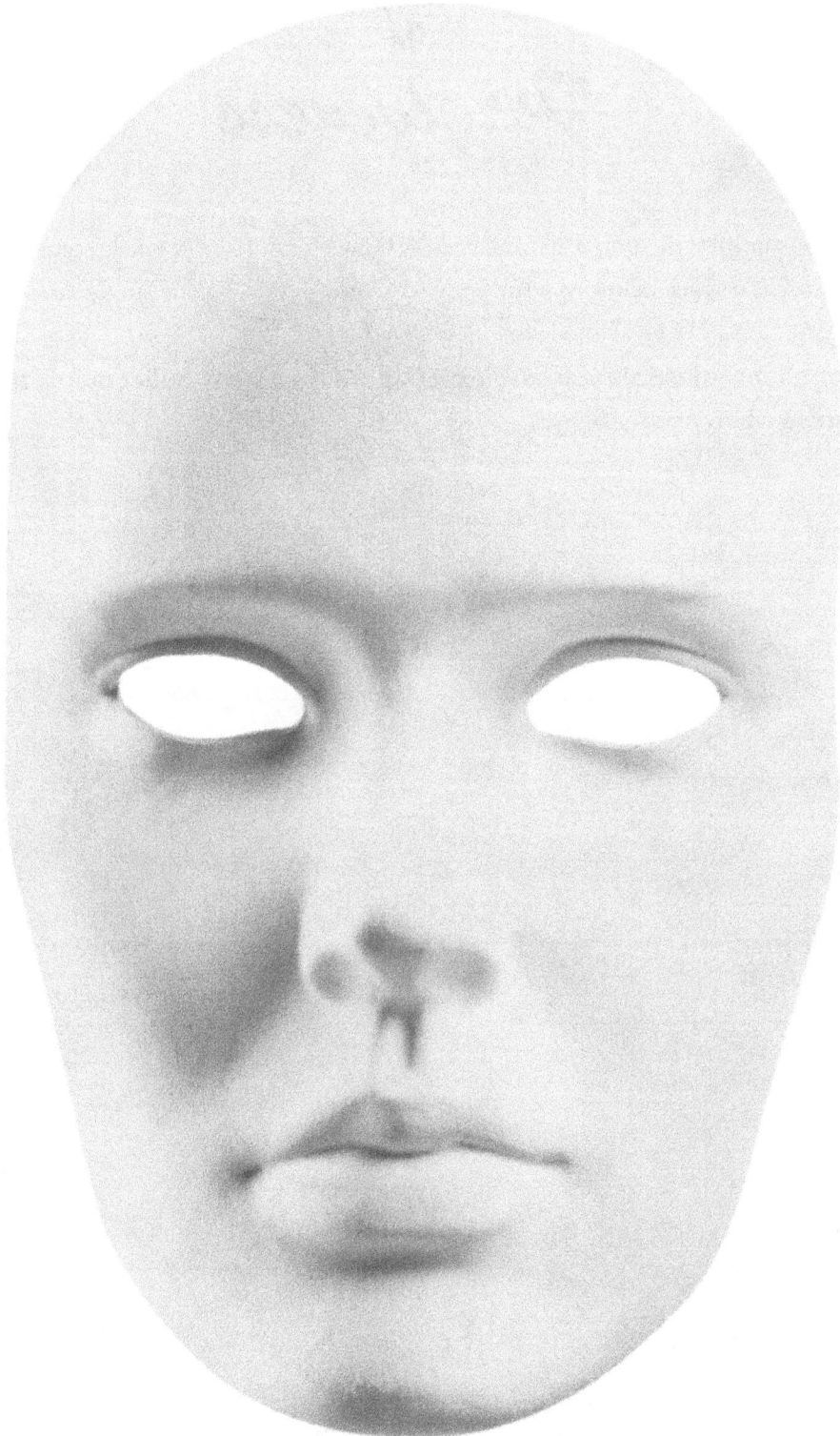

Template 7:
Forgiveness List

the Process

of

Forgiveness

You will now look at how the personal injustices you have endured in your lifetime have affected you. **On your own,** use the space below to write your reflections. Revisit your 'anger' list.

Make a list of all the injustices you have experienced. Just write bullet points for example, 'My parents divorced when I was a baby.'

1. ....

2. ....

3. ....

4. ....

5. ....

6. ....

7. ....

8. ....

9. ....

10. ....

11. ....

12. ....

13. ....

If you need to add more 'injustices', continue writing in your notebook if necessary

'Bring & Share' – Forgiveness Exercise

For this part of this exercise, you must be specific and write the **name(s)** of those who have been unjust towards you, i.e. Uncle J, etc. I have divided them into categories to help you. Continue with a separate sheet if you need to. If in a group, take **five** minutes to complete this list on your own first. Once completed, share it with your peers. Share your reflections with your group or a sister in Christ. **Please do not write full names in the interest of privacy.**

Loved Ones

Brothers & Sisters

Place of Work/Study

Communities/ Nations/Others

Template 9

My Heartfelt Letter to Christ.

Dear Yeshua,